Name It What
You Feel

Anita Nezhad

Dedication

To those who have loved, lost, and still found the strength to love again.

To those whose hearts have been shattered countless times, yet with every wound, they have learned to love even deeper.

To the silent keepers of love—those whose hearts are filled with untold stories, whispered only to the stars, never heard by another soul.

To the dreamers who believe in the magic of emotions, the power of words, and the beauty of an unbreakable heart.

And to you—wherever you are, whoever you may be—may this book be a companion to your heart, a light in your moments of doubt, and a reminder that your love, your story, and your feelings are beautifully valid.

Acknowledgment

This book would not have been possible without the unwavering support and encouragement of those who have touched my life in countless ways.

To my family and friends—your love, patience, and belief in me have been the foundation of my journey. Thank you for always standing by my side, through every high and low, and for reminding me that dreams are worth chasing.

To my readers—you are the heartbeat of this story. Your kindness, enthusiasm, and connection to these words give them life. I am deeply grateful for each of you.

To my father, whose soul is always with me—your love, wisdom, and strength continue to guide me, even from beyond. Though you are no longer physically here, I feel your presence in every step I take. Thank you for believing in me, then, now, and always.

And to Kitty, my beautiful, fluffy companion, who has taught me the true meaning of unconditional love—pure, boundless, and given without expectation.

With love and gratitude,

Anita Nezhad

Contents

Introduction

Sometimes life unexpectedly drags us into darkness. In those moments, no matter how hard you try to escape, something inside holds you back. This story is about one of those moments, a moment when everything seems to be working against you, yet in the end, that same darkness becomes the spark for a glimpse of light.

Life is a game, and awareness is the key to success in this game.

Chapter 1

A Magical Night

I glance at the mirror one last time, adjusting my hair with a careful hand. A faint smile creeps across my lips, everything must be perfect tonight. This is the night I have been waiting for, the one I have counted down to for a whole year.

A year ago, when I bought my ticket for the Coldplay concert, I did not know how I would endure the anticipation. But now, after twelve months of dreaming, the wait is finally over. My heart is racing faster than ever, ready to lose itself in the rhythm of the music.

The moment feels almost surreal. Just a few more hours stand between me and the night I have imagined so vividly. As I slip into the simple yet special outfit I picked for this occasion, it feels like I am preparing for a meeting that could change my life forever. Every detail of this evening holds meaning for me, the hum of the music in my mind, the glow of imagined lights, and the moment when Chris Martin's presence will illuminate my world.

As I step out into the night, the cool breeze brushes against my face, carrying with it a mix of excitement and nervous anticipation. Tonight is the night when all my dreams might just come true.

My love for these enchanting melodies and heartfelt lyrics was so deeply woven into the fabric of my soul that even the unimaginable felt entirely possible.

Following that enchanting night, I found myself lingering in the radiant, colourful world it had left behind, carrying its magic with me throughout the week. With a heart brimming with gratitude and passion, I shared words of thanks, hoping to return even a glimmer of the boundless love and joy their music had gifted me. That night, without me realizing it, marked the beginning of a profound transformation in my life.

It was a night like no other. The anticipation had built up over an entire year, and as I stood in the crowd at Allianz stadium, surrounded by thousands of voices singing along, I felt like I was part of something transcendent. The stage came alive with bursts of colour, the pulsing rhythm of "a sky full of stars," and Chris Martin's voice cutting through the noise, clear and raw.

The energy was electric, coursing through every soul in the stadium. Strangers became friends in an instant, united by the magic of the music. I could feel the vibrations in my chest, the bass syncing perfectly with my heartbeat.

As the song reached its crescendo, Chris paused, letting the crowd carry the melody. Thousands of voices rose in unison, filling the night with something that felt almost sacred. I closed my eyes, letting the moment wash over me—pure, unfiltered joy.

When I opened them, the stage was bathed in soft blues and purples, as if the universe itself had come down to join us. Chris spoke to the crowd, his words simple but filled with gratitude. "You are not just fans, you are part of this. Thank you for making this night unforgettable."

And unforgettable it was. The night stretched on, song after song, each one carrying its own wave of emotions. "Fix You" brought tears to many eyes, the lyrics cutting deep into unspoken feelings. "Viva La Vida" turned the stadium into a pulsing, singing sea of light and movement.

For a few hours, the outside world disappeared. No worries, no stress—just music, light, and connection. The music flowed through the infinite expanse of existence like a sacred rain washing away all sorrows and grief. In those moments, I wished that everyone in the world could be there, hand in hand, celebrating this beauty and harmony together.

I closed my eyes and found myself like a phoenix, spreading its colourful wings, ready to soar. I flew through the silver sky of the night, accompanied by shining stars, and together we glided over this earthly sphere, sharing our love with all. In that pure and precious moment, there was only one wish in my heart, to share this endless love with everyone.

When I opened my eyes, the magic of the night still lingered in my heart. The stage was bathed in soft hues of blue and purple as if the universe itself had descended to join us. Chris looked out at the crowd, a smile on his face.

That night was more than just a concert, it was a moment of pure human connection, a celebration of life, love, and the power of music to unite us all. For those few magical hours, our heartbeats became one. I wished it would never end.

But fate had other plans for me.

It all began when, aboard the ship of belief, I ventured to the planet of love, a journey that felt like stepping into a dream. And then, the moment arrived. The name "Martin" appeared on my phone screen, as though the universe itself had sent me an invitation and it had just been confirmed.

From that day forward, my world changed, and life revealed a side of itself I had never imagined. It was hard to believe, almost surreal, but it was him, Chris Martin.

For years, his music had been the soundtrack to my life. Each song carried a memory, each lyric a moment frozen in time. Through the highs and lows, his magical melodies had been my companions, offering solace, joy, and reflection.

And now, as if the stars had aligned, he had stepped out of the realm of melodies and into the simplicity of my world. It felt as though a dream had crossed the boundary into reality. A journey I never thought possible had begun.

Chapter 2

A Dream Come True

A magical week had passed, each day overflowing with joy and a sense of wonder, it felt like a memory etched forever in my heart. I found myself scrolling through their pages, captivated by their journey across this vast planet. Each photo, and each video, brimming with love exchanged between the band and their fans, filled me with an indescribable sense of excitement and connection.

Amidst this sea of emotions, I stumbled upon a video of Chris. He spoke about their upcoming plans, his words carrying a familiar warmth. He mentioned that although they rarely engaged with social media, they had recently decided to be more active online.

The video, casually recorded on a phone, felt intimate and personal, as though he was speaking directly to me. Moved by his words, I decided to leave a heartfelt comment, a simple thank-you, and a glimpse into the emotions his music had stirred within me.

Comment:

Thank you, for coming to Sydney! Thank you for giving us unforgettable memories and for leaving a piece of your beautiful spirit with us.

Your music and energy fill us with so much joy and inspiration. We are grateful for every beat, every lyric, and every moment you share. Cannot wait to see you again.

You are amazing, guys!

Beneath the concert posts, hundreds of heartfelt comments overflowed with love and admiration. It felt as though we had all come together, sharing our purest emotions in one beautiful, collective moment.

Some of the comments had received replies, though the responses were hidden. All you could see were fans expressing their gratitude with words like, "Thank you, Chris," or, in some cases, longer and more expressive messages.

I could not help but think, how lucky they were, Chris noticed and replied to them. A quiet hope stirred within me, if only he would see my comment too, and perhaps, leave me a reply.

A few days went by, as I carried on with my peaceful, uneventful life. But then, one day, as I was checking my emails, something unusual caught my eye and stopped me in my tracks.

"Thank you for your love and support, it means the world to me. I am endlessly grateful for each and every one of you. Your messages fill my heart with joy and inspire me every single day.

If you would like to share more love or just say hello, feel free to drop me a message through the link below. I cannot wait to connect with all of you! Sending much love your way."

So, when he responded to my message

- His words appeared in my inbox.
- It felt like a miracle, like the universe had reached down and whispered, here is your moment.

My heart leaped as I read his kind and thoughtful reply. For the first time in what felt like forever, I was seen, heard, and acknowledged by someone I deeply admired.

At first, it was just a simple exchange-a thank-you for my heartfelt comment.

But as days passed, our messages grew longer, and more personal. He shared pieces of his life, his thoughts, and his dreams. He asked about mine. I could not believe that someone like Chris, someone I had watched from afar, could take such genuine interest in me.

In those moments, I was not thinking about fame or distance. I was not thinking about what was realistic or rational. I was thinking about how alive I felt. The world seemed to glow in softer hues, like a song playing just for me.

Overcome with an overwhelming surge of joy, I could not hold my laughter, the sound spilling out uncontrollably. I leaped into the air, my heart racing, as I read the message again and again, each word lighting up my soul. Almost as if drawn by an invisible force, my hand moved to the magical link. With a single click, it felt as though I had stepped through a doorway into an entirely new and enchanted world.

The irresistible allure of forbidden fruit, luscious and tempting, its sweetness calling out to you, yet the moment you reach for it, you risk tasting the bitterness of its hidden poison.

The moment the first message appeared in my private inbox, it was as if I had been swept away into another world, a place where I felt unmoored, with nothing to ground me.

They: Hello, dear. Can you please tell me your name and where you live?

Me: Hi, I am Anna, and I live in Sydney.

They: Nice to meet you, Anna. I saw your comment and wanted to thank you. I must admit, out of all the comments, yours stood out to me the most.

Me: Thank you for your kindness.

I remembered the moment those messages were exchanged. I had such a strange feeling. I did not know if it was Chris himself or just a group admin replying on his behalf. But whoever it was, I was happy. I was thrilled that my message had been read, and that I had received a response.

They: Can you tell me how long you have been a fan of our band?

I started describing the day I first heard Yellow, pouring my feelings into every word, reliving the moment as vividly as I could. I felt like a child, lost in wonder, turning a simple birthday into the grandest, most dazzling celebration in their imagination, sharing it with their father, the one they loved more than anyone else, hoping he would see the magic through their eyes.

They: Wow, you amazed me. That is why your comment caught my attention more than the others, I must admit. You have very delicate feelings. So, I made the right choice.

I replied with a heartfelt smile, "Thank you," and sent a smiling emoji.

They: You're welcome. I have to say, your energy feels so warm and unique, even through words. That is rare to come by these days. I am the lucky one to notice it.

I asked, "May I please know your name?"

I was brimming with excitement, like a child awaiting their bottle of milk—tiny hands reaching out, feet kicking with anticipation, their whole being alive with the promise of warm, sweet comfort. Impatient yet overjoyed, they let out soft, endearing sounds, a melody of pure delight.

Instead of answering, they responded with a question of their own.

They: Could you please send a picture?

This question made me doubt it.

Who is this person, an admin, Chris?

Me: Are you the admin of the group?

For a moment, I stopped typing, my eyes glued to the Telegram screen.

They began typing. I could see the movement of his hands on the keyboard, represented by the three little dots dancing on the screen. My heart raced as I waited for his next words.

They: I just want to know who I am talking to. Do not feel pressured, though.

His response brought a deep sense of calm to my heart, but I was still conflicted inside. Could it be him, or was this just a game?

At that moment, the next message arrived instantly.

"No, no, I am Chris," he said.

My eyes were glued to the screen, my breath hitched, and I swallowed hard.

"Are you Surprised?" he added, with a smiling emoji.

With trembling hands, I typed and erased my words over and over, completely unsure of what to say. In the end, I kept it short.

Me: Yes, I am surprised.

For several minutes, I could not bring myself to reply, words failed me. I felt the heat rising in my cheeks, a vivid blush spreading across them. The rhythm of my heartbeat, loud and steady, was the most beautiful music I had ever heard. It was a sensation so fresh, so profoundly enchanting, that it took my breath away.

Me: "You're very kind. Maybe that's why you're so loved."

Chris: "Being loved isn't something you chase; it's just a result. But I always try to stay human."

With those last words, I felt like maybe he was who he said he was.

Although doubts still lingered in my mind, I wanted to believe that such a conversation with someone like him was possible.

Without a second thought, I opened my photo gallery. It felt as though my hands were no longer mine to control, they belonged entirely to my heart, which seemed to guide their every move.

I have never thought of myself as photogenic, so I searched carefully for the best picture I could find. Finally, I selected one, clicked, and sent it.

It is just a picture; it is no big deal, I told myself. Yet, even with lingering doubts, I wanted to hold on to this wonderful feeling. I wanted to believe.

Chris: "Wow, you are incredibly beautiful, just as I imagined. May I ask if you are single or married?"

His question made me pause and doubt for a moment. I knew he was engaged, and this was not something someone in his position would typically ask. It felt like a question someone single might ask.

Me: I am divorced, and I have a son.

He responded almost instantly.

Chris: I would like to get to know you better if you are open to it.

My heart felt like it was about to burst out of my chest.

My hands were damp with sweat, and I had not anticipated anything like this. A strange discomfort settled over me.

I decided it might be best to change the subject. Even though I already knew where he was from the concert schedule, I asked anyway, hoping to shift the mood.

Me: Can I ask where you are right now?

Chris: New Zealand.

Then, after a pause, he asked me again: Would you be open to getting to know each other better?

When he said that, I paused for a moment, thinking to myself, maybe it's just the admin trying to mess with me, or maybe he's being a little playful. I laughed quietly, amused by the thought. This cannot be serious, right?

Without thinking too much, I replied, "Yes, of course. We can be good friends. It would be an absolute honour to be friends with you."

Chris: "That's great, but what I meant by getting to know you more is something beyond just an ordinary friendship."

I read his message and smiled, thinking it might be some kind of joke or even a playful game meant to entertain me for a few minutes. But then, he assured me that he really was Chris. His words carried a surprising confidence, and for a brief moment, I found myself caught between disbelief and curiosity.

Or maybe… he is just trying to be playful, someone who wants to enjoy a lighthearted conversation away from the pressures of fame and the public eye. I chuckled again, thinking how surreal it felt to be talking to someone who claimed to be Chris Martin. If it is a game, it is a fun one, and I do not mind playing along for now.

Trying to mask my confusion, I replied, "I am not sure what you mean. Could you explain a bit more?"

Trying to keep the conversation light, I replied with a playful tone, "I am not sure what you mean. Care to explain a bit more?"

I leaned back, a grin forming on my lips as I watched the typing indicator flicker. Is he going to keep up this little game? The thought amused me.

Just then, my phone buzzed with an incoming call. I declined it without hesitation, I was not about to let anything interrupt this curious and oddly entertaining exchange. I waited, intrigued, wondering what he would say next.

Finally, this message came through.

Chris: "I have always wanted to experience life like an ordinary person and to be treated as one. Something about you tells me you could give me that feeling. I want to get to know you better if you are willing. I truly mean this."

I smiled, amused by how surreal it all felt. Is he serious? Or is this just another playful twist? Before I could fully process it, another message popped up:

Chris: "Of course, I do not want to put any pressure on you. I just feel like the universe has brought us together here for a reason. Nothing in this world happens by accident."

His words reminded me of The Alchemist by Paulo Coelho, a book I had read countless times. The idea that nothing is a coincidence was something I had always believed in. But could this really be one of those moments? I was not sure, but it made me curious.

I took a deep breath, trying to stay composed as I watched his "online" status frozen at the top of the screen. Could this be a message from the universe? I thought, still smiling.

Without hesitation, I opened Google and searched for any news about him and his fiancée. Surely, if they had broken up, it would have been all over the news by now, right? But no. Every article painted a picture of a strong, loving relationship.

I frowned, feeling a mix of curiosity and amusement. Is this part of the game? Or is something else going on?

I walked into the kitchen, poured myself a glass of water, and took a sip. It did not help much, so I poured another. Taking a deep breath, I tried to shake off the strange feeling. Relax, it is just a conversation, I reminded myself with a smile.

When I opened Telegram again, the blue "online" indicator had turned grey.

Still smiling, I began typing:

"Can I ask you a question?" and pressed send.

Moments later, his reply came through:

Chris: "Of course. I told you to feel comfortable with me. You can ask me anything."

I hesitated for a moment, then typed:

"What about your fiancée? I know you are engaged. This feels a bit strange, and I would not want to disrespect anyone."

I hit send and watched as the typing indicator flickered on and off. It felt like he was typing, removing, and starting again, making me wonder what he was struggling to say. Finally, the message arrived:

Chris: "Yes, I know it looks that way in the media, but the reality is different. It is all because of my career, it has to be that way. I've never truly experienced real love, and I cannot explain more than that. So, your answer is no, right? I hope you understand."

For a moment, I felt an odd, almost foolish excitement bubbling inside me. Could this really be happening? All those years of listening to his music, daydreaming about him, and now he was here, talking to me. It felt like a dream slipping into reality, too strange to believe yet too tempting to ignore.

I laughed quietly, remembering how just a few weeks ago, life had felt overwhelming. I had sat alone in my room, drained and exhausted, wondering if things would ever change. And now, here I was, caught up in a bizarre but oddly thrilling situation.

That day, I was speaking to the universe, or perhaps, the universe was speaking to me. If you think I will break, you are wrong. I have faced enough to know that giving up is not an option. Even if I must walk alone, I will not abandon my kindness or integrity. Test me, I will rise.

Now, in the quiet aftermath of that memory, it felt like the universe had finally answered.

I had always trusted my heart. It never lied. To me, true wealth was not in possessions but in the values, I held—kindness and truth.

Yet, deep down, there was a shadowed corner in my heart, a place I rarely visited. Perhaps, I was not ready to face what lay there.

With a deep breath, I began typing:

Me: "Alright, if that's truly how it is, then we can get to know each other better."

I paused for a moment, wondering if he had left the conversation. Did he get bored? Or maybe he's busy? The thought of losing his attention briefly crossed my mind, but I quickly brushed it off with a quiet smile. If this is meant to happen, nothing can stop it. That belief had always grounded me.

Minutes passed without a reply. I placed my phone aside and turned on some music, letting the soft melody fill the air. I leaned back, feeling oddly at ease as if everything would unfold in its own time.

In my mind, I became a vibrant, colorful bird, soaring freely from one place to another. It was a rare and pure feeling, something I had never experienced before.

As the music played, I went about my daily tasks, but everything felt different. I moved with ease as if guided by an unseen rhythm. It was as though a long-extinguished lantern deep within me had suddenly reignited, casting its warm glow over everything.

A joyful warmth spread through my body, making me feel truly alive. I sang along with the music, my voice stronger and freer than ever, as if I had been given a song by the universe itself.

Just then, the soft chime of a message brought me back to reality.

His face appeared on my screen, radiant and captivating. Golden curls framed his moonlit skin, and his ocean-blue eyes seemed almost unreal. The colours felt richer, and more vivid, as if painted just for me.

With a racing heart, I opened the message.

Chris: "I'm so glad you said yes," he wrote, followed by a warm smile. "Now, tell me, what do you dislike, and what do you love?"

Excitement bubbled up as I typed:

"I despise lies and betrayal, and I adore truth and honesty."

With a deep breath, I hit send.

Chris: "It seems we've found our first common ground," he replied, adding another smile. "I, too, despise lies and betrayal. For me, honesty and sincerity are the foundation of everything meaningful in life. Humanity and truth are the most precious treasures. Compassion and kindness are at the core of who I am. But tell me, do you think people can ever change completely, or do they always carry some part of their past?"

His question caught me off guard. I paused, reflecting on his words before typing:

"I believe people can change, but only if they truly want to. Some parts of the past will always remain, but they do not have to define who we are."

Chris: "Wise words. I agree. I have spent my life trying to grow beyond the image the world has of me. It is exhausting at times, but necessary."

As I read his message, I felt a sudden, undeniable connection. It was as if he was voicing my own thoughts. This was exactly what I had always longed for, someone who shared my deepest values and understood the complexity of life.

Every day, I tried to grow, to accept my mistakes, and become a better person. All my initial doubts had vanished. There was no room for hesitation anymore; I was utterly convinced it was truly him.

The thought that this could be anything else did not even

cross my mind. Everything around me felt brighter as if bathed in a golden glow.

I felt light, almost weightless as if I had been lifted above the chaos of the world. A laugh escaped my lips—free, unrestrained. I raised my hand in silent gratitude, thanking the universe for this unexpected moment.

Without overthinking, I typed:

"I am proud of you and truly grateful for people like you. You inspire more than you probably realize."

I hesitated for a second, unsure if I should say more. My mind was a whirlwind of emotions—excitement, wonder, and a hint of disbelief. I could not help but smile as I stared at the screen, waiting. The rhythmic dance of the three dots felt hypnotic, each flicker carrying a promise of something extraordinary.

Finally, his message appeared:

Chris: "If you have any questions, feel free to ask, do not hesitate. But honestly, most of what you want to know about me is already online. People like us do not have privacy; we are always on display.

But enough about me, I would love to know more about you. What do you do, and who do you live with?"

Lying on my stomach on the floor, a smile permanently etched on my face, I quickly typed my reply:

"I perform miracles on people's skin, I turn tired faces into fresh ones and sometimes even convince wrinkles to take a vacation! Oh, and by the way, I live with my son and a little fluffy cat."

Chris: "Wow, sounds like magic! I might need one of those miracles for my skin," followed by a smile.

Me: "Of course, it would be an honour! Just let me know when you are ready for your transformation."

Chris: "So, what else do you enjoy? I mean, how do you usually spend your free time?"

Me: "I love reading and writing poetry. I enjoy philosophical and simple books, and I am passionate about animals and tennis."

Chris: "It is amazing how similar we are. By the way, I write all my songs myself, but I guess you already knew that."

Me: "Of course, I knew! You have always had a way with words. That is why your songs feel so real."

Chris: "And what about tennis? Do you play?"

Me: "I do! And just so you know, if we ever play a match, I will win. No offense."

Chris: "Oh really? You think you can beat me? I might surprise you with my hidden skills."

Me: "Hidden skills, huh? Well, bring it on! But I am warning you, I play to win."

Chris: "Challenge accepted! Now I am curious. We should definitely play someday."

We both laughed. Even though this was just a playful conversation, it felt strangely real, as if we were actually planning a match. The idea of competing with him made me smile, and for a moment, it felt like the line between reality and fantasy had completely blurred.

Chapter 3

The Beginning of Love

Even though I am usually a quiet person, every moment of this conversation made me feel more excited. For once, I did not want the dialogue to end, I could have talked to him forever.

Me: "I also do charity work."

Chris: "Wow, really? Tell me more."

Me: "I collect clothes and supplies for people in need, and I also send food and medicine for animals."

Chris: "That is incredible, another thing we have in common! I have a charity too. Honestly, as a public figure, it is kind of expected, but I do it because I genuinely care. It is a big part of who I am."

Me: "That is amazing! I love doing this kind of work, it brings me so much joy. Not long ago, I helped save a young man's life. He needed money urgently, and without it, things could have ended badly. It felt incredible to make a real difference.

Oh, by the way, if you have any clothes, a guitar, or maybe even a piano lying around that you do not use, let me know, and I will come pick them up for charity!" followed by a wink emoji.

Chris: "Haha! I will check, but I am keeping my guitar, it is off-limits! Still, I love your spirit."

Me: "Fair enough. But do not be surprised if I show up one day asking for a donation!"

Chris: "Deal! Just let me know when, and I will have something ready."

Chris: "What's the plan for today?"

Me: "I just moved into a new house, so I'll be spending my day unpacking boxes and trying to make sense of the chaos."

Chris: "Do you like your new house?"

Me: "Yes, it is much better and bigger. Plus, it has enough space for my cat to run around like a queen!"

Chris: "That is great! Sounds like you have got your hands full."

Me: "What about you? What is your plan for today?"

Chris: "Actually, I was about to tell you, I must go. We have a practice session with the band."

Me: "Alright, I will not keep you any longer. It was nice talking to you."

Chris: "Do not mention it. I am glad I got to know you."

Me: "I know you are super busy, so I will try not to bug you. Just text me whenever you are free. But do not forget, I am waiting for that tennis match!" followed by a wink emoji.

Chris: "Haha, deal! I will not forget. Talk soon."

Chris: "Thanks for understanding. I will always make time for you."

Me: "Thank you. I hope you have a wonderful day. Take care of yourself."

Chris: "Thank you, you too," followed by a heart emoji.

For a moment, I noticed Chris was typing. I did not want him to leave yet. My eyes stayed glued to the screen until his message popped up:

Chris: "Can I ask you to keep this between us? Please do not tell anyone. My position is sensitive, and no one can know about this until we figure things out. Can I trust you?"

Me: "Of course. You can trust me."

Chris: "Please, promise me. It's not easy for me to trust, I have been hurt too many times before. I need to know you mean it."

Me: "I promise. Trust is everything to me, and I would never betray it. I know how it feels to be hurt, and I would never do that to someone else."

Chris: "Thank you. I am really grateful."

Me: "No need to thank me. I am here. Whenever you want to talk, I will be around."

Chris: "I will. Talk soon, I will always make time for you."

I could not stop smiling, my lips stretched into a grin that just would not go away. I sat there, staring at his blue "online" status like a kid waiting for the ice cream truck, making sure it did not vanish before my eyes. When it finally turned grey, I let out a breath, I did not realise I was holding.

His last message kept echoing in my mind, making my heart race:

"I'll always make time for you."

I sighed, then burst into laughter. You silly girl, calm down! A warm, fuzzy feeling spread through me, and I felt lighter than air.

Still grinning like a little girl who had just been told she was a princess; I turned the music back on and got back to unpacking. But my ears stayed alert, ready for the faint ping of a notification. Control yourself! I whispered. But how? How can I when this feels like a dream?

At one point, I gave up. I sat down, grabbed my phone, and started watching Chris's interviews, his mannerisms, his voice, his smile.

It was him. It was really him. Chris.

My world felt like it had been turned upside down, bathed in a magical glow. I felt like a little girl in a fairy tale, waiting for her first dance at the ball. And in my mind, tiny, glittering fairies whispered, what gown will you wear for your first date?

The weight of 45 years disappeared, and I felt like a 14-year-old girl experiencing her first crush. Standing in front of the mirror, I tilted my head, inspecting my face.

"Hmm, not bad... but seriously, I need a facial." I ran my fingers over my cheeks and added with a grin, "Maybe a miracle too."

Leaning in closer, I frowned at my teeth. "God, these teeth! Braces would be nice. Nelly was right all along." I chuckled, remembering how my sister never missed a chance to point it out.

I gave myself a playful wink, fluffed my hair, and whispered dramatically, "Okay, princess, time to shine! Let us start by unpacking these boxes, and maybe fixing you up a bit along the way."

I turned on my favorite Coldplay playlist, letting the upbeat rhythm fill the house. With every box I unpacked, I could not help but dance, twirling and swaying to the music. At one point, I grabbed a nearby spoon, held it like a microphone, and started singing at the top of my lungs.

Danny peeked out of his room, giving me a puzzled look. "Mom... are you performing a concert or something?"

Grinning, I struck a dramatic pose. "Obviously! Care to join the audience?"

He rolled his eyes, laughing as he closed the door. "You're crazy."

Crazy or not, I felt fantastic. The house felt brighter like the music was infusing every corner with energy and hope. For the first time in a long while, everything felt new, like I was standing at the beginning of something wonderful.

By the time dinner was ready, I was still buzzing with excitement. Sitting at the table, I barely touched my food, impatiently waiting for the moment I could check my phone for messages.

Finally, the moment arrived, but that night, there was no word from Chris. Instead, sleep claimed me, carrying me into dreams.

In my dream, I wore wide-legged, ash-grey pants torn at the knee and a white T-shirt splattered with vibrant paint. My long, wavy hair flowed freely as I sat quietly in the corner, watching Chris and his band rehearse Viva la Vida. Softly, I sang along under my breath, the music wrapping around me like a warm embrace.

The feeling was magical. I danced and sang all night in my dreams, waking up several times, impatient for the morning to come.

At 4:35 a.m., I finally gave up on sleep. The sky outside was still dark as I got out of bed. Kitty, my fluffy companion, followed me downstairs, her soft paws barely making a sound.

I made myself a cup of coffee, my eyes glued to my phone, hoping for a message. Nothing. With my coffee in hand, I stepped onto the balcony. The cool morning breeze kissed my face as I stroked Kitty, her gentle purring breaking the silence. Still no message.

Trying to shake off the impatience, I took a cold shower. The water was invigorating, washing away my restlessness. Feeling refreshed, I dried my hair and reached for my phone again.

And then, there it was, Chris's face lighting up my screen. My heart skipped a beat as I quickly unlocked my phone, my hands trembling with excitement.

Chris: "Good morning, Anna. I hope you did not miss me too much." He added a smiling emoji.

Me: "Good morning, Chris. I will not lie, I did miss you."

His reply came almost instantly:

Chris: "I missed you too. Even during practice yesterday, I could not stop thinking about you. There is something about you, something fresh and uplifting. It feels… different. In a good way."

My heart raced, and warmth spread through me, impossible to contain. Without thinking twice, I quickly typed back:

Me: "I feel the same way," adding a smiling emoji.

Chris: "Could you send me another picture of yourself?"

I grinned, thinking for a moment. Instead of a serious photo, I quickly snapped a funny one, making a silly face and holding my cat like a lion. I sent it, laughing to myself.

Me: "Here's one to make you smile!" followed by a laughing emoji.

Chris: "Haha! You are hilarious. I needed that laugh. But seriously, you are beautiful, send me a proper one too."

Still giggling, I sent him another photo, this time a simple one with a smile.

Chris: "Wow, you are absolutely beautiful. I am so lucky to have found you," followed by a heart emoji.

I felt a rush of giddiness as if my whole body was glowing. Smiling to myself, I replied:

Me: "Thank you! You are making me blush—I'm shy," adding a shy emoji.

For a moment, I wanted to ask, could you send me a picture of yourself too? I longed to see him right then, to imagine him sitting behind his phone, smiling as he talked to me. But I hesitated. What if he says, 'My pictures are everywhere on the internet?' The thought made me feel silly, so I let it go.

I was still lost in my thoughts when the sound of a message pulled me back to reality.

Chris: "What would you do for me if we decided to be together?"

I froze, his words echoing in my mind like the lingering notes of a song. I could not fully grasp what was happening. Just as I tried to gather my scattered thoughts, another message appeared:

Chris: "When I said I wanted to get to know you better, I meant every word. I am a man who stands by his promises. I do not say things I do not mean. I am waiting for your answer."

His words left me breathless. Before I knew it, I was swept into a vivid daydream—us, walking barefoot along a sunlit beach, the golden sand warm beneath our feet. His hand in mine, steady and reassuring, while the ocean breeze played with my hair. The waves whispered softly to the shore as we moved in perfect harmony, the rest of the world fading away.

Lost in that dream, I felt my heart swell with something pure and undeniable. It was as if, in that moment, the line between dream and reality blurred.

With that feeling deep in my heart, I began to write my reply, letting sincerity flow from every part of me:

Me: "When we are together, we will not be two separate souls, we will be one. I will cherish you as deeply as I cherish myself. I will dedicate myself to bringing joy into your life because that is what I have always dreamed of doing for the one I love."

Chris: "Thank you. Your honesty and sincerity mean the world to me. The more we talk, the more I believe the universe brought you into my life for a reason. Your words radiate love, I feel it deeply."

Me: "You're welcome. I always speak from the heart. Whatever lives in my soul finds its way into my words."

I was just mustering the courage to ask him something when his next message popped up:

Chris: "Darling, ask me anything. I want you to feel completely at ease with me."

Oh my God, can he read my mind? I thought, both surprised and amused.

Before I could reply, another message appeared:

Chris: "I want you to trust me, and I beg you, never betray me. Can you promise me that?"

In my mind, I saw myself standing before him, gently holding his hands. His skin felt soft, like a soothing night breeze. Gazing into his ocean-blue eyes, I whispered:

"I would never betray love. Love is sacred, it's the essence of who we are. I love myself, and in loving myself, I embrace love in its purest form. How could I ever betray something so divine?"

I watched the blue "online" indicator glimmer softly,

knowing he was reading my message.

My eyes were closed, but I could see him clearly as if he were right beside me—seated on a light-colored couch, a soft smile playing on his lips. His eyes, steady and thoughtful, were fixed on the phone screen, absorbing every word I had written. His fingers moved gracefully, and the subtle dance of three dots flickered on the screen, promising a reply.

I held my breath, calm and steady, as if the world itself had paused to listen. There was a strange, weightless feeling in my chest, a blend of anticipation and something more profound. And then, his reply appeared:

Chris: "I feel like I am falling in love with you, a love I have never known before. A pure love. You are so beautiful, not just outwardly, but in your soul. I feel incredibly lucky to have found you."

My heart raced wildly, like a stallion galloping through an endless green meadow, its mane swept by the wind, its gaze fixed on the horizon. My hands froze mid-air, my eyes moving back and forth across his words as if scanning them for hidden meanings, for something more. I swallowed hard, trying to steady the whirlwind inside me, but every deep breath only heightened the trembling anticipation.

At that moment, I knew, I had fallen in love. A love that was tender, pure, and undeniable. I longed to be near him, to hold him close, to rest my head against his shoulder and whisper, "I feel the same, I truly do."

Lost in that dream-like moment, I suddenly noticed the blue "online" light fade to grey. He was gone. I had waited too long.

Panic surged through me, and I found myself whispering, "No, please, don't go." Without hesitation, I typed back:

"I feel it too. I think I have fallen in love, a love so unfamiliar, so beautiful, like nothing I've ever known."

Then, as if carried by the rush of my emotions, I sent him a verse from Rumi:

"The beauty you see in me is a reflection of you."

Suddenly, in my mind, I found myself in the room where Chris and his band were rehearsing. He sat at the piano, his fingers gliding effortlessly over the keys, while I stood beside him, reciting softly:

Wherever I turn, it is you that I find,

In rustling leaves and the wandering wind.

The sea takes its depth from the thought of you,

The desert its calm from your silent hue.

In your gaze, time fades away,

The world stands still, its moments stray.

You are the root of all that is real,

The pulse of life, the fire I feel.

Stay with me, love, through shadow and light,

Through fleeting dawn and endless night.

Let the rain cleanse body and soul,

Until we are one, forever whole.

When the rainbow splits the skies,

Our hearts will soar where colors rise.

No start, no end, no passing time

We are light, eternal, and sublime.

The room felt alive with music, every note echoing the emotions in my heart. Chris played on, his eyes briefly meeting mine, a soft smile gracing his lips. It was as if, at that moment, the entire world had faded, leaving only us—two souls bound by something pure and unspoken.

Chris: "Thank you, that is so beautiful. I love it."

"I must go now, but I promise I will message you as soon as I can. For now, you write to me, I will always have time for you."

(With a smile.)

I did not want to let him go. Quickly, I started typing:

Then I will write to you every day, just like Judy Abbott in Daddy-Long-Legs. Have you read her story?

Chris: "I might have read it, but I would love to hear it from you.

It is the story of a girl who writes letters every single day to a man she has never met. She imagines him in her dreams and lovingly calls him Daddy-Long-Legs.

Chris: "How interesting! (Smile emoji)

Chris: "I will call you Sunshine because you've truly brought light into my life like the sun."

As my entire being glowed like the sun itself, my breaths flowed softly and steadily from my chest.

I said: Sunshine is beautiful—I love it. (Heart and smile emoji)

Chris: I am glad you like it. (Heart and red rose emoji)

My hands froze over the keyboard, my mind struggling to find a name worthy of him. I knew it had to have "blue" in it—blue, my favourite colour, the colour of the sky, the ocean, and the eyes of my love, where I saw a reflection of myself.

The blue "online" light had turned grey, he was gone.

I could see him with the band, standing behind the microphone, rehearsing. He tuned the instruments, ensuring everything would be perfect.

Meanwhile, I sat in a quiet corner. I loved sitting on the ground, my headphones in, my long, wavy hair spilling around me, my knees tucked up to my chest. My poetry notebook was in my hands as I searched for a beautiful name for him.

I whispered to myself as I wrote:

"Blue Star? Blue Ocean? Blue Bird? Blue Sky?"

As I sat there, unable to take my eyes off him, I softly whispered the names under my breath. Then, "Blue Sky" gently flowed from my lips. He seemed to me like the Blue Sky—endless, majestic, and serene. Blue, my favourite, symbolised the ocean's depth and the boundless expanse of the heavens.

I sat quietly in a corner, watching him as my words flowed effortlessly onto the screen.

Night had draped its velvet-black, star-studded cloak over the Earth. I stretched out on the ground, letting the warmth of Mother Earth seep into my skin. The air was heavy with the intoxicating fragrance of jasmine, and I lay there, mesmerized, gazing up at the heavens. The stars twinkled like scattered diamonds, their lights dancing like Christmas fairy lights.

Among them, one star stood out—brighter, more radiant,

almost otherworldly. I reached out toward it, and its luminous glow travelled through my fingertips, cascading down my body, and flooding me with light. In that ethereal moment, we became one, wrapped in a celestial embrace.

"To my Blue Sky, with love," I typed, feeling each word as if it were etched into my soul, and pressed send. I added softly:

"Your name is now Blue Sky," followed by a heart emoji.

I waited for a few moments, my heart racing in anticipation of his reply.

He sat at the piano, his fingers gliding over the keys as he played and sang with effortless grace. Then, as if sensing my gaze, he turned to me with a mischievous wink that sent a spark through the air. Enchanted, I held his gaze, my eyes brimming with love, and offered him a soft, tender smile. To seal the moment, I slowly blinked a silent gesture of approval and affection, letting my heart speak through my eyes.

I stepped back slightly, noticing how perfectly organized my wardrobe had become. A soft smile tugged at my lips as I glanced at my phone. The music filled the room, creating a sanctuary of peace, and I was blissfully lost in my beautiful world.

But then, a small notification caught my eye, I had not noticed that another message had arrived.

This time, it was a voice message. My heart skipped a beat. Could this be happening?

In the fleeting seconds between clicking and hearing the message, countless questions flooded my mind. Had he sent me one of his most beautiful melodies? Could it be a short piece he had sung just for me?

Finally, as I held my breath, my heart racing, my brain allowed my finger to press the button.

Chris, with that mesmerizing voice of his, said:

"Hey Sunshine, my beautiful Sunshine. I just wanted to tell you that you have not left my mind for even a second. I have been thinking about you the whole time."

For a brief moment, I saw him clearly in my mind—standing up from the piano during his break. He walked toward me, sitting by the rehearsal room, his eyes locked on mine. Taking my hand, he quickly pulled me along, my hair swirling around as we moved. He led me to his workspace, shut the door behind us, and pressed me gently against the wall by the door, his intensity taking my breath away.

His gaze intertwined with mine, a knot of eternity formed in his eyes, impossible to untangle. The warmth of his breath brushed against my skin, tender and unyielding. His hands moved like the gentle caress of waves upon the shore, ebbing softly only to return with a quiet intensity.

And then, as his voice barely escaped his lips, whispering, "My beautiful Sunshine, I love you," his lips found mine, binding us in a kiss that felt like poetry itself—endless, profound, and destined.

I was still lost in the magic of his words when the next message arrived:

"I want to hear your voice. I want to know what my beautiful Sunshine's voice sounds like."

His words sent a wave of excitement coursing through me. I could not stop smiling as I replayed his message over and over, it was his voice, speaking directly to me.

What should I say? I wondered, my heart racing. I pressed the voice message button, recording and deleting my attempts several times, each one feeling less than perfect. Finally, I decided to keep it simple and let my feelings speak for themselves.

I sent my reply:

"Hey, my blue sky. I have been thinking about you this whole time too.

Without a moment's hesitation, I sent him a picture I had taken on the bus, on my way to a concert. Along with it, I wrote:

"After so long, taking the bus feels so nice. Heading to a concert.

Chris: "What a beautiful photo. Riding the bus... is something I truly miss.

Me: "Do not worry. One day, I will do your makeup so flawlessly that no one will recognise you. We will hop on a bus together, and when we reach the ferry terminal, we will get off and board a ferry to Central Park. There, we will kick off our shoes and run barefoot across the soft grass, as far as our lungs will let us, until we collapse, laughing, and lie down on the earth's green carpet. We will gaze up at the sky, surrounded by the sound of water fountains, the melody of the wind, and the playful dance of birds, all bathed in the shimmering rays of the sun."

As we lay on the grass, the wind played gently with the blades, weaving through our fingers like a soft melody. Our eyes were fixed on the endless blue sky above, watching the clouds drift by in a puppet show of nature's creation. The scent of wildflowers mingled with the earthy aroma of the soil, and the distant song of birds floated through the air, carried by the playful breeze. Everything felt alive as if the world itself was breathing with us.

Chris broke the silence, his voice warm and contemplative. "What a beautiful world we live in. We're so lucky to be a part of it."

I smiled, my gaze still on the clouds. "A world filled with beautiful, colorful things," I replied softly, feeling the warmth of the moment seep into my soul.

Chris turned to me, his eyes shimmering with a kind of quiet wonder. "A world overflowing with love."

I nodded, my heart full. "Love is the greatest wealth any human can possess," I said, my words coming from a place deep within.

Chris's fingers gently traced the grass beneath him, as if trying to connect with the earth itself. "It's the best feeling," he said, his voice tender. "Love might be just an emotion, but within it lies an entire universe—a boundless, infinite world."

I whispered back, "Love is breathtakingly beautiful when dressed in humanity. It is in the small acts, the moments that remind us of who we are."

Chris's gaze returned to the sky as he spoke, his voice growing softer, almost reverent. "Love is everywhere if only we take the time to see it. In the birth of a child, in the radiant smile of a homeless person when you give them a gift. It's in the soft stroke of a hand on a stray animal's fur, in the gentle twist of ivy creeping up a garden wall, in the colours of a rainbow stretching across the sky after the rain."

I closed my eyes for a moment, letting his words wash over

me. The breeze kissed my cheeks as if agreeing with him, and the world around us seemed to hum with quiet affirmation.

"Time feels different here," I said, my voice barely above a whisper. "As if this moment doesn't belong to today or yesterday, but to something eternal."

Chris smiled, a look of peaceful contentment on his face. "Moments like this remind us that we are part of something bigger, something infinite. Love, kindness, the beauty of life… they are all part of the same story."

I turned to him, my heart swelling with gratitude. "Maybe that's what makes life so magical—the way love finds its way into the simplest things, the smallest corners of the world."

We fell silent again, the sound of the wind, the rustling of the leaves, and the faint murmur of a nearby stream filling the space between us. In that moment, we were not just observing the world— we were part of it, wrapped in its beauty, its love, its endless possibility.

Chapter 4

Unfolding Destiny

As I typed, I could picture it all so vividly, as if we were already there, living that perfect moment.

Chris, hesitated, typing and erasing his response a few times before finally sending it:

"Wow, that was incredible. You know, you write so beautifully. Why haven't you turned this talent into a career?

I said, "I tried many times, but unfortunately, life kept taking me in a different direction, and I had to let it go. But now, I am writing it for you." And I sent a smiling emoji.

Chris: You should not let go of it. You have a gift, one that can paint worlds more real than reality itself.

I smiled as I read his words. For a moment, I forgot where I was sitting in my quiet room, the faint hum of life outside my window, and instead, I felt as if I were sitting across from him, sharing a secret that only we knew.

Me: Thank you. But sometimes life is not about what we want; it is about what we must do.

Chris: That is true, but maybe it's time to start fighting for what you want. You never know who is waiting to hear your words.

His response stayed with me longer than I expected. You never know who is waiting to hear your words. Could he be one of those people? Was he trying to tell me something? I pushed the thought aside. After all, this was not real, was it?

Me: Maybe you're right. I have been waiting for someone to remind me.

Chris: Well, here I am. Your biggest fan. Now, tell me more. Where do we go after Central Park?

I paused. My fingers hovered above the keyboard, and suddenly, the words flowed as if they had been waiting for him to ask.

Me: After Central Park, we will stroll through the city streets, stopping at a small café with a crooked sign and tables painted in faded red, as if they carry the stories of everyone who sat there before us. We will order two cups of coffee—yours, black and strong, and mine, sweet with cream. We will sit by the window, the glass fogged slightly from the warmth inside, and watch strangers pass by, weaving their own tales through the streets.

You will tell me about your favourite song, and as you speak, your eyes will light up like the melody itself. I will hum a tune, one you have never heard before, but as you listen, it will feel like it has always been a part of you, like a memory from another life.

As the day turns golden, painting the streets with soft amber light, we will walk back toward the water. The sun will bow to the horizon, its reflection dancing on the waves, kissing them goodbye. And there, as the sky blooms into shades of purple and pink, I will remind you that moments like these do not need fame or fortune, they just need two hearts brave enough to believe in them.

For a long while, Chris did not respond. I worried I had said too much, but then:

Chris: You have no idea how much I needed to hear that today. Thank you.

At that moment, I felt as though I had given him a piece of the dream we were building together, one message at a time. But what I did not realise was that in giving him a dream, I had unknowingly created a space for myself to hope again.

That day unfolded beautifully by Chris's side. I had left everything behind—my worries, my doubts, even my real name, Anna. It felt as though I had been reborn, carrying a new identity, a new light, in the name he had chosen for me: Sunshine.

Chris asked me to write something beautiful for him every day and send it to him. He told me he would share it with his influencer network and assured me that my book would eventually be published. His words carried a weight that made my heart race with excitement and disbelief. Could this really be happening?

Then, as if to seal the dream, he added something even more surprising: he offered to use his name and influence to support me.

"I'll help you get your book out there," he said, his tone warm and sincere. "But promise me, you'll keep this between us, like a secret, until the right time comes."

The weight of his trust and generosity overwhelmed me. The thought of my words being shared with the world, my book finally published—it felt like magic. But the secrecy he requested added an air of mystery, as if we were guarding a treasure only, we could see.

I took a deep breath, my fingers trembling as I typed back.

"I promise, Chris. This will stay just between us."

As I sent the message, a small voice inside me whispered doubts. Was I being too naive? Was this too good to be true? But the hope in my heart drowned out the voice of caution. For now, I chose to believe him. I chose to believe in the dream he was offering me.

A few moments later, he messaged again, letting me know he had a meeting to attend. He explained that in a few days, he would be travelling to London for a charity event at a church, something that required careful planning with the band's manager.

Before leaving, his words took on a tender, romantic tone.

"I'll miss you, Sunshine. Wait for me, okay? I'll message you as soon as I am done."

His message lingered on my screen, filling the room with a warmth I had not felt in years.

I replied, assuring him that I would wait for him and expressing how proud I was of him for dedicating his time to such meaningful causes. I told him how inspiring it was to see someone using their platform to make a difference, and that it only made me admire him even more.

All my daily tasks were falling apart as if I had become a stranger to my own life. I lied to my son, telling him I was busy searching for a new job and applying for positions. In reality, I was too preoccupied to focus on anything else, resorting to feeding him sandwiches and prepackaged meals, feeling guilty with every passing day.

The night before he left for the church event, we were talking softly, the conversation drifting into a more intimate realm. There was something about the way he spoke to me gentle yet intense that made me feel like he saw parts of me no one else had bothered to look at.

Out of nowhere, his voice turned low, almost hesitant, as though he was revealing a vulnerable part of himself.

"Can I ask you something? How long have you been… alone?"

The question caught me off guard. My heart fluttered, my

breath hitching slightly. I hesitated, but there was something safe about his voice, like a warm hand reaching out in the dark.

It has been years, I admitted softly. But it is not just about being alone. I am not someone who can be with someone for just one night. I cannot share that part of myself unless I care deeply… unless I love.

There was a pause on the other end, and for a moment, I wondered if I had said too much. But then his voice returned, soft and deliberate, carrying a weight I had not expected.

I am the same, he said. I could never do that with someone I did not care about. For me, it is not just about the physical act it is about the connection.

His words wrapped around me like a silk thread, delicate yet binding. I could almost see him sitting there, imagining the scene he began to paint for me.

For me, it is about trust, about knowing the person in front of me is not just a body, but a soul I have fallen for. I imagine us lying there, in the quiet of the night, where everything else fades away. Just two people breathing each other in, every touch meaningful, every kiss a promise. It is not about desire alone it is about feeling like you belong somewhere, in someone's arms, completely safe.

I closed my eyes, his voice lulling me into a vision I could not escape. I saw it so clearly soft light filtering through a window, the world outside forgotten. His hands found mine, fingers interlacing slowly as though there was no rush, no need to hurry. The heat of his skin, not just against mine, but sinking deeper, until it felt like he was touching my very soul. It was not frantic or fleeting. It was steady, tender, and real two people finding something they had not known they were missing.

My cheeks burned as I opened my eyes, the silence hanging between us heavy with unspoken thoughts. My heart was racing, and I wondered if he could sense it even across the distance.

Finally, he whispered, that is what it is meant to feel like. I hope you know, I would never want anything less with you.

The honesty in his voice left me breathless as if he had reached across the void between us and touched something deep inside me. I wanted to say something anything but all I could manage was a quiet, thank you for saying that.

That night, I lay in bed long after our conversation ended, staring at the ceiling, and replaying his words over and over. For the first time in years, I let myself dream of what it would feel like to belong to someone like that not just in body, but in heart.

I felt the gentle dance of his hands on my skin, like the morning breeze tenderly caressing the delicate petals of spring blooms. The warmth of his kisses on my lips was the golden sun spilling its light across the tranquil blue of the endless ocean. We burned together with a fever a sweet, intoxicating fever born of love. The rhythm of our hearts, beating as one, composed a melody more beautiful than any song, weaving poetry into the silence of the night.

And as we drifted into a deep, peaceful sleep, I whispered to my soul: if this is but a dream, let me sleep here for eternity.

I was drifting in a deep dream, far away from the noise of the world, when the warmth of a soft kiss stirred me awake. Slowly opening my eyes, I saw Kitty, my little fluffy cat, her tiny tongue brushing against my face. It was her daily ritual her way of pulling me back to reality, eager for breakfast and a bit of playtime. Smiling, I ran my hand over her silky fur, pressing a tender kiss to her head before reaching for my phone.

The screen lit up. It was 6 a.m., and as always, it was cluttered with emails and notifications that meant nothing to me. My heart raced, searching for just one message the one I was waiting for.

And there it was. A video from Chris.

I opened it quickly, and there he was—his face radiant, soft as if bathed in the light of the moon. His voice, smooth and warm, filled the silence of the early morning.

"Good morning, sunshine, my love. Thank you for making

me feel this way. Thank you for treating me like just an ordinary man, not someone on a pedestal. You have given me something I did not know I was missing."

He paused, his smile deepening, his eyes soft.

"I love you."

At that moment, the entire world seemed to fade. All that remained was his voice, his presence, and the pounding of my heart echoing the words I had just heard.

The video messages he sent would vanish after a single viewing, and I understood why. His position demanded caution; his world was one where trust was both rare and fragile. He had shared with me, more than once, the betrayals he had suffered wounds that still lingered in his heart. It was as though each betrayal had taught him to build higher walls, and he had made me promise, repeatedly, to keep what we had a secret something just for us, untouched by the world outside.

I remember one evening when his voice grew quiet and reflective, he told me about a piece of advice his mother once gave him:

"Be careful not to let your ship spring a leak, because once it does, it's bound to sink.

Her words hung heavy on him, a reminder of how easily everything could fall apart if trust were misplaced. I could see it in the way he carried himself cautious, and guarded, yet longing to feel safe. And so, I honoured his fears, his wounds, and his need for privacy.

For him, for us, I would keep this delicate secret safe, as though it were a precious treasure I had been trusted to protect.

I was still lost in my thoughts when another message popped up, a photo of him, playfully blowing me a kiss. His beard was slightly grown out, and underneath the photo, he had written: "Do not worry, I am off to shave now." He had added a small, cheerful smile emoji.

My heart melted at the sight of his photo, and I wrote back:

"You are perfect in every way." Along with a heart emoji.

Chris: Send me a photo right now.

Caught off guard, I felt a wave of nervousness. I was not ready at all no makeup, just a simple t-shirt. I replied.

Me: I am not ready for a photo right now. I promise I will send one later.

Chris: I just want to see the love of my life in this moment. Do not worry, My Sunshine. You are in my heart, and I do not care what you are wearing or whether you have done your makeup. What matters to me is you. Please, send it.

Once again, he gently pleaded, look, I sent you a simple

photo, even though my job does not allow it. But I trust you completely, so please trust me too.

At that moment, I realised he was right. It was not about trust; I trusted him with all my heart. I was just embarrassed. I was not good at taking photos, and I never thought I was photogenic. But then I told myself, let whatever is meant to happen, happen now.

Finally, I gathered the courage to take a selfie. After snapping and removing countless photos, I managed to find one that looked decent enough. I sent it to him, along with a kiss.

He replied instantly.

Chris: You are absolutely beautiful. The more I get to know you, the more I am convinced the universe brought you into my life, as if I was meant to find my true love right here. Tell me, how do you feel about us?

I was overjoyed by his response and quickly replied.

Me: Thank you! I feel the same way. It is like we are both on the same energy wavelength I can feel it so strongly.

Chris: I wish you were here with me. These past few days, I have not stopped thinking about you, not even for a moment.

Me: Maybe you should stop thinking about me and just place me in your heart instead.

I could not resist being a little playful with him.

Chris: You are the queen of my life.

Me: And you are the king of mine.

We spent what felt like an eternity exchanging tender words, sharing photos, and scattering romantic emojis back and forth. By then, the night had fully embraced the world, wrapping it in darkness.

Chapter 5

First Doubts

I found myself wishing, more than anything, to be with him. I imagined us lying side by side on the cool earth, gazing up at a sky ablaze with stars. I would stretch my hand toward the heavens, and he would place his hand gently over mine. Together, we would rise, weightless, into the night, soaring past the clouds, searching for our star, the one that shone brighter, pulsing with life, calling only to us.

We would settle upon its luminous surface, bathed in its silvery glow, and in that celestial light, we would become one bound forever in the infinite expanse of the universe.

That night, the air was icy, and snowflakes tumbled from the heavens like luminous pearls, swirling gently as if in a celestial dance. It was as though Mother Earth had draped herself in a stunning white wedding gown, shimmering in the moonlight.

The fireplace flickered softly, casting a warm glow across the room. I stood in my grey turtleneck sweater, feeling the cozy embrace of its knit, and called out to Chris.

Me: Darling, I am almost ready. How about you?

Chris, buttoning up his sleek black coat, glanced at me with a smile.

Chris: I am ready too.

Hand in hand, we stepped into the snowy night, a soft crunch underfoot as we walked toward one of the city's finest restaurants. A private table awaited us, reserved just for the two of us. The evening unfolded like a dream specialty dish crafted by the chef, with decadent desserts, and impeccable service that made every moment feel extraordinary.

That night, our words flowed like a love song, weaving a tapestry of laughter, tenderness, and sweet confessions.

On the drive home, the magic lingered. With love songs playing softly in the background, we sang along together, laughing and teasing each other, even slipping into playful silliness. The snow continued to fall, its delicate dance illuminated by the glow of the headlights, wrapping the world in a quiet, ethereal beauty.

I spent the entire night dreaming of him, imagining the warmth of his skin and the soft rhythm of his breath brushing against my face.

A gentle smile formed on my lips, and without thinking, I reached out to touch his face. But to my surprise, oh my God, it was not him. It was Kitty, my fluffy little cat!

The morning had arrived, and there she was, licking my face with her tiny, scratchy tongue as if trying to wake me up. I could not help but laugh, planting a quick kiss on her head before reaching for my phone.

Like every morning these past few days, my heart raced as I searched for one message and there it was.

A voice message from Chris arrived:

Good morning, my sunshine, my beautiful love. You were with me all through the night.

The smile on my lips was unshakable as if he could see into my very thoughts. Without hesitation, I replied with my voice message:

Good morning, my beautiful blue sky. I was with you all night and I will always stay by your side.

I quickly began writing a piece for him in my poetry journal:

Dawn bathed the world in golden light,

Love's soft kiss banished the night.

Birds in song, the sky did gleam Whispered tales of every dream.

Your hands, my shelter, calm and true,

My restless soul found peace in you.

Eyes locked deep, the world stood still,

Time surrendered to our will.

Drunk on you, we touched the skies,

Held by sunlight's warm disguise.

Winds sang softly in our ear,

Dreams of love drew ever near.

Clouds became our tender bed,

Where hearts as one, with love were fed.

In your arms, the world did fade,

Only love's eternity stayed.

At the end, I wrote:

With love, for my one and only, my blue sky.

Chris: This is perfect, my beautiful sunshine. You are not just beautiful on the outside but inside too. I feel so incredibly blessed to have you in my life. Heart emoji.

Chris: I want you to send me a photo, but this time, I want to see your entire beautiful figure.

His request completely caught me off guard. I had never even imagined he would ask something like that. For a few moments, I froze, unsure of how to respond. This was something I had never done before I was far too shy.

And then, another message arrived:

Chris: My dear Sunshine, do not be shy. I know you are a little reserved, but don't you trust me? You are my queen, aren't you?

Then he sent me a photo of himself at the beach, wearing nothing but swim trunks, and followed it with another message:

Chris: There are countless photos of me shirtless online. Don't I deserve the chance to see my queen, the love of my life, without clothes? Is that too much to ask?

I was completely stunned. After taking a moment to collect my thoughts, I replied:

Me: Yes, of course, you have the right. Just give me a little time. I have never done anything like this before. Blushing emoji

Chris: My love, I know you are shy, and I understand. But please know, I cannot wait forever. Still, for you, I will try to be patient.

Then, he said he had to leave, mentioning he had a busy day ahead. As always, he sent me a photo and a kiss before saying goodbye.

My breath hitched, and my heart pounded wildly in my chest. What should I do? What kind of photo should I send? The questions swirled in my mind.

Frantically, I opened my photo gallery, scrolling through old pictures of me in bikinis, but it was obvious they were outdated. Unsatisfied, I turned to my wardrobe, pulling out a few old outfits I had saved from my younger days. None of them fit anymore.

I searched through everything, determined, until I stumbled upon a bikini Nelly had gifted me long ago one, I had never even worn.

It was a stunning two-piece, black and pink, elegantly decorated with delicate white lace and tiny seashells. Sophisticated and undeniably sexy.

Over the past few days, Nelly had sent me several messages, but I kept my replies short to avoid raising any suspicion. Each time, I made some excuse about unpacking boxes or organising things before quickly ending the conversation.

I could never lie to her I was terrible at it, and besides, she was far too sharp and intuitive. If something were off, she would figure it out in an instant.

Nelly, my beautiful sister, always looked out for me and supported me just as I did for her.

I slipped into the bikini and stood in front of the mirror, taking in my reflection. It was breathtaking. For the first time, I could not help but admire myself. The combination of black and pink, accented with delicate seashells and white lace, created a striking contrast against my sun-kissed skin.

I let my long, wavy hair cascade around my shoulders, playfully tossing it from side to side as I captured several photos in the mirror. Each one was more beautiful than the last.

It was the first time, I deeply appreciated and enjoyed my beauty.

I chose the best photo, and with my hands trembling, I hesitated for a moment before sending it. Then, I took a deep breath.

I waited for a reply for a few minutes. When nothing came, I set my phone aside and focused on my tasks. I was behind on so many emails that needed replies, and I had a few calls to make. I tried to immerse myself in my everyday life, even if only briefly, though it was not easy. My thoughts and heart were still with Chris.

After about two hours, a message finally arrived:

Chris: Wow, my beautiful queen, my sunshine, you are stunning. Your beauty is truly admirable, I must admit.

(with a few hearts and kiss emojis)

Each time he praised and admired me, it felt as though something new blossomed in my heart, like the delicate unfolding of a flower bud at the break of dawn on a serene spring morning. I felt the warmth of the sun radiating within me, and my eyes sparkled like a dazzling diamond. I gave a brief reply:

Me: "Thank you."

Chris: "I must leave for London tomorrow for a performance at a church. I need to get everything organised before I go because I want you to be here, when I return."

My heart pounded wildly, steady, and loud, like the resonant chime of a church bell.

Me: All right, when will you be back? What date should I book a ticket for?

Chris: I am not sure about the return date yet. It depends on my manager's schedule. But as soon as I know, I will arrange the ticket for you.

Filled with excitement, I replied: Okay!

Chris: Just one thing, I cannot meet with fans without my manager's approval. Do you have the Black Membership Card? It is exclusive to our band.

I had never heard of such a thing before and felt a wave of embarrassment and confusion wash over me. I thought to myself, how could you not know about this?

Me: No, I do not have a membership card. What is it, and where can I get one?

I quickly turned to Google, searching for answers, but nothing came up. There was no information about this membership card anywhere online. I scoured every site I could think of, only to come up empty-handed. Just then, another message came through:

Chris: You need to purchase it from my official office in London.

I was even more confused now. I did not want to lose this chance, so I kept searching, and trying different websites, but there was no trace of an official office or anything about the card.

Chris continued messaging:

Chris: It is a bit pricey, but you should be able to pay for it, right?

I felt a mix of confusion and unease. A membership card just to meet him? And now I was expected to pay for it? My mind raced with countless unanswered questions.

I asked him: "What is this card for?"

Chris: This card is for private meetings with my fans, which must be approved by my manager. It allows fans to meet me through an official process.

I sign off on the date and time to decide which fans I want to meet. Once you purchase it, your name and details will be registered in my office, and I will sign off to dedicate that day entirely to you.

I was a bit confused, but at the same time, it seemed somewhat reasonable. I did not reply.

Chris: Of course, once you purchase this card, you will not need to buy it again. After that, it will be up to me to decide. The price is €1,500.

Chris added: Of course, I will help you too.

His words brought me some comfort, but the fact that I could not find anything about this Black Membership Card on the internet made me suspicious.

I asked, "All right, where can I get it? Can you please share the official website for the Black Membership Card?"

Instead of answering my question, Chris said: "How much can you pay? I will cover the rest."

I repeated my question, but no response came. Once again, I started searching online.

I felt lost and decided to search for Chris's official office in London, hoping I might find some information about this Black Membership Card on their website. But again, nothing came up. How was that even possible? I typed in every phrase I could think of, yet there was no trace of it anywhere. Frustration and doubt began to settle in.

Chris messaged again: Just tell me how much you can pay, and I will take care of the rest.

My mind stalled for a moment. Why should I have to pay for a membership card just to see the person I love? It did not make sense. Shouldn't he be the one covering the cost, especially since the card was supposed to belong to him? Questions piled up, unanswered and unsettling.

Finally, I gathered the courage to ask:

Me: Why would you have to pay for a membership card that is supposed to be yours?

Chris's reply came quickly, and his tone carried a hint of irritation, he said, "Because, I am not just an ordinary person. Why don't you understand? I cannot meet my fans without following protocol. I wish you could see that. I do not know why I must explain everything to you. You do not trust me at all."

He went on by saying, "I have risked everything in my career, and my reputation just to be with you. I have sent you videos and voice messages every single day, even though I am not supposed to. My love for you made me break all those boundaries. And now, you are questioning me? If you do not trust me, just say so right now. I cannot accept love without trust."

His tone made it clear that he was genuinely angry. For a moment, I felt a pang of shame deep within me.

I still had not received a clear answer to my question, but his response had left me both shocked and uneasy. A deep fear crept in, what if he decided to leave me? I felt lost, unsure of what to do. At that moment, all I wanted was to hold on to him, no matter what.

I quickly typed a reply:

Me: Hey, my blue sky, did I upset you?

And then, I waited.

The hours stretched on, and by nightfall, there was still no response.

Stress and anxiety consumed me as I kept checking my phone, hoping for a reply that never came.

That night, no message came. Sleep was impossible. I spent the whole night checking my phone over and over again, hoping for something, anything. My mind was a storm of fear and uncertainty. All the doubts I had about the membership card were now forgotten, replaced by a single, overwhelming fear, what if he left me? What if he never replied again?

I scrolled through Telegram repeatedly, making sure I had not been blocked or deleted. Each time, the silence felt heavier, like a weight pressing on my chest. My thoughts spiraled uncontrollably, conjuring up endless scenarios, each one worse than the last. I felt powerless, trapped in the silence of his absence.

It was near dawn when I finally closed my eyes, utterly defeated and drained. Sleep came in fragments, and like every other morning, Kitty's soft licks pulled me back to consciousness. My heart raced as I grabbed my phone, desperate for any sign. And then I saw it, a message.

Chris: Yes, I am upset. I feel like you do not trust me, and for me, trust is the most precious thing in any relationship.

My hands trembled as I typed back, almost pleading:

Of course, I trust you. I just must admit, I have been a little confused.

I quickly added:

Please do not stay upset with me, I am begging you. Please, my blue sky, do not let this come between us.

I was desperate to soothe his anger, to win him back. I even tried to add a playful, affectionate tone, hoping to soften his heart and bring a smile to his face.

I sent him a beautiful song by the legendary Demis Roussos, "Forever and Ever (You'll Be the One)."

It was a song my father used to sing to my mother, one filled with so much love and meaning. It had always held a special place in my heart, and sharing it felt like offering a piece of my soul.

At that moment, I imagined him listening to the song, his face lighting up with a gentle, beautiful smile as the melody wrapped around him.

Forever and Ever

Ever and ever, forever and ever

You'll be the one

That shines in me

Like the morning sun

Ever and ever, forever and ever

You'll be my spring

My rainbow's end

And the song I sing

Take me far beyond imagination

You're my dream come true, my consolation

The reply finally came:

Chris: It was a beautiful song, really lovely.

Me: So, does this mean you are not upset anymore?

Chris: Hmm… not quite satisfied yet.

Me: What can I do to make it up to you? I sent a big kiss emoji and added, "Are you happy now?"

Chris: Alright, I will forgive you this time.

Me: Great, now send me a smile.

Chris sent a smile emoji.

Me: Okay, now tell me what I need to do.

Chris: Do about what?

Me: I mean about the membership payment.

Chris: Here is how it works. Tell me how much you can pay, because the payment needs to come from your account for it to register in the system. I will handle the rest.

Me: Why don't you just send me the website link so I can pay directly?

Chris: You are not getting it. From my end, I need to input your name and details into the system, and a part of the payment needs to come from your account. Tomorrow, when I go to London, I will finish everything from my office.

He paused and added, "Send me your full name, phone number, and email address so I can create a file for you right away. I know this is a big risk for me, but I am willing to do anything to make this happen and see you."

I quickly typed out all the details he had asked for and immediately checked my bank account. There was $565 in it, and my next payment was not due until the following week. I had taken two weeks off work because of the move, which had already left me stretched thin.

I could not bear to tell him I did not have much money, nor did I want to risk losing this chance. I reassured myself, thinking, I will just borrow the rest from Nelly if I must.

While I was still deep in thought, a message from Chris

popped up:

Congratulations! Your registration is almost complete. Are you ready for the next steps?

I quickly replied: Thank you so much. Yes, I am ready.

But the truth was, I was not ready. A lingering doubt hovered in the back of my mind, though I could not quite figure out its source. His words still felt unclear, and many of my questions had gone unanswered.

I had asked him several times for a link or access to the official account, but each time, he managed to steer the conversation in a different direction.

In the end, I told myself to stop overthinking and decided to just go along with whatever he asked.

Chris repeated his question yet again:

How much can you pay?

Feeling nervous and flustered, I blurted out: $500.

Chris: Alright, do you have a bank card?

My anxiety made me freeze for a moment, completely forgetting which card I had. I quickly grabbed my wallet, checked, and typed: Visa card.

Chris: Great. Now, take a photo of it and send it to me both the front and back, please.

He continued, "I will talk to one of my trusted staff members and let you know."

I replied, "Sure."

Within me, clouds of fear loomed, casting shadows of doubt over the vast expanse of my dreams. I kept searching on Google, tirelessly scrolling, yet no matter how deep I delved, I found nothing.

I replayed our conversations over and over in my mind. It was like a puzzle whose pieces stubbornly refused to fit. For a moment, I stepped into his shoes and asked myself, if you were him, what would you do?

A man of such wealth and status, why would he ask me how much I could pay? Even if I had said $2,000, would he still have accepted it without question? If it were truly just for registration, couldn't he have simply said, "Transfer $20, $40, or even $10?" But he did not. Not a word. Why?

Chapter 6

A Beautiful Illusion

Fear had taken hold of me, wrapping itself around my thoughts like a dark fog. Yet, despite the growing unease, my heart clung stubbornly to the sweet, intoxicating taste of love, refusing to let my mind step in and unravel the illusion. It was as if my heart, desperate to hold on, had silenced my reason and locked it away.

I felt like even my heart could no longer find peace. Desperately, I began searching, Google, YouTube, and Instagram, and then, suddenly, something caught my attention.

A new video had been released that very day on Coldplay's official Instagram channel, featuring Chris and the band. In the video, Chris explained that they would be performing at an event in a church in London in a few days.

My heart skipped a beat as I realised this was the very event Chris had mentioned to me during our conversations. For a moment, it felt like confirmation proof that everything he had said was true. Seeing this brought a small sense of relief to my anxious heart as if it were clinging to this detail as evidence that my trust was not misplaced.

That night, I nervously checked my bank account, half

expecting to see something missing. But to my surprise, nothing had been withdrawn. Relief flooded through me, but it was quickly followed by a heavy wave of guilt. How could I have doubted him?

I felt ashamed, as though my suspicion had betrayed the bond, I believed we shared. And yet, beneath the surface, a faint, unwelcome whisper of doubt lingered a shadow that refused to disappear entirely, no matter how much I tried to silence it.

The next morning, as had become my habit in those days, I checked my phone the moment I woke up. No messages.

I reassured myself, thinking he must be busy with preparations for the upcoming event at the church.

Still, I could not resist sending him a message.

Me: Good morning, my blue sky. Wishing you a day as beautiful as your heart.

I added a heart emoji and a kiss emoji, hoping to brighten his day as much as he had brightened mine.

That day, I wrote to him:

I wandered through the emerald fields of my life's most cherished memories, where the silver lake of my experiences lay waiting. The radiant sun of my breath bathed its surface in golden light. Gently, I dipped my feet into the water, seeking the tender gift of its kiss, a moment of pure bliss.

Upon the lake's tranquil mirror, a boat began to drift, as weightless as a feather on the breeze. It bore a flag of gold, adorned with a single, resplendent heart. As the boat neared, I saw, with growing clarity, my blue sky reaching out his hand to me from within.

And then, as if summoned by the heavens, a bird sang sweetly in the air:

A gift from the cosmos. A gift from the cosmos.

With all my heart, I dedicate this to you, my only blue sky.

I waited. Minutes turned into hours. My phone screen remained blank, no reply lighting it up with the warmth I had grown used to. I told myself not to overthink it. He is busy, of course he is.

But doubt had a way of creeping in, like a cold draft under a locked door. By midday, I could not stand the silence anymore. My mind churned through possibilities—was he hurt? Overwhelmed? Or worse... had he seen my message and decided to ignore it?

To distract myself, I threw myself into chores, but every little sound from my phone had me rushing to check, only to be greeted with notifications from apps I did not care about. By evening, the unease had transformed into a sharp pang of worry.

Finally, just as the stars began to dot the sky, a message appeared.

Chris: Good evening, my darling. I hope your day was filled with as much love as you give. Apologies for the delay, things have been a little hectic on my end.

The relief that flooded me was overwhelming. My fingers trembled as I typed out a reply, eager to erase any impression that I had doubted him.

Me: I am just so happy to hear from you. I missed you today. I hope everything is okay on your end. Always here if you need anything.

As I sent the message, my heart softened. His words had a way of disarming my fears, making me feel foolish for doubting him in the first place.

Chris: I am leaving for London early tomorrow morning, but before I go, I want to make sure everything is perfectly set for us to meet.

Overwhelmed with joy, I could hardly contain myself.

Me: Absolutely! I will do everything I can to be ready.

Chris: What about your son? Will he be alright? Do you have someone to look after him? I want you to be completely at ease when you are with me. As a father myself, I truly understand your situation.

His words resonated deeply with me, touching my heart in a

way, I had not expected. I could not help but think how noble and compassionate he was, someone who even considered the well-being of my son.

I knew nelly was coming back from her trip next week. During our last conversation, she had asked to stay with us for a while so she could save some money. She was determined to work hard, and together, we decided to sell the old house our father had left us as an inheritance. With the money, we planned to buy a larger home in a better neighbourhood, where the three of us could start a new chapter together.

Me: do not worry, I have got someone who can look after him. Leave it to me.

For some reason, I could not bring myself to mention my sister, nelly. Even up until that moment, her name had never crossed my lips.

He read my message, but no reply came.

Excitement coursed through me, filling every corner of my being. The thought of finally meeting my beloved made my heart race. I could not focus on anything else. I began planning what to pack, making sure I would not forget a single thing that mattered.

Just as I was lost in my thoughts, his next message arrived:

Chris: I cannot wait to see you, my sunshine.

Me: And I cannot wait to see you, my blue sky.

At that moment, my heart felt like it was soaring. Everything felt surreal, like a dream I did not want to wake up from.

Me: Did you manage to pay for the member card?

Chris: I am so sorry, I have been incredibly busy and completely forgot. I will check on it today and let you know. I must go now, it is a hectic day, and I need to get ready for my trip.

I recalled he had mentioned leaving that morning, but I did not dare to ask further. Maybe he is just overwhelmed, I told myself, choosing not to press him. Instead, I simply said goodbye and, as usual, ended the message with a kiss and a heart emoji.

I walked to my wardrobe and began pulling out my best outfits, one by one. Holding each piece up in front of the mirror, I pictured myself wearing it next to Chris. But deep down, I knew I wanted to keep it simple I wanted to show up as my true self.

I finally chose the outfit I had worn to the concert: a pair of loose, smoky grey jeans with uneven rips over the knees and a T-shirt with vibrant splashes of colour on both the front and back, set against a soft green background.

As I laid the outfit on my bed, Danny's voice echoed from his room. He was immersed in his video game, his shouts of excitement breaking the quiet.

I froze for a moment, a wave of worry washing over me. Oh God, what am I going to do about Danny? What should I tell Nelly? I had never travelled alone before, and I had always shared everything with Nelly. She was my rock, the most dependable and trustworthy person in my life, always supporting me no matter what.

I knew I could not deceive her, nor could I bring myself to lie. The thought weighed heavily on me, but I resolved to call her, even though the stress gnawed at me like an unrelenting shadow.

At last, I mustered the courage to dial her number, though my mind was still a whirlwind of uncertainty. I felt trapped between two impossible choices; to lie to Chris or to lie to Nelly.

I whispered to myself, let fate take its course. If something is truly meant for you, no force in the world can take it away.

With those words, I calmed my racing heart. I took a deep, steadying breath and, summoning every ounce of bravery, I called Nelly.

Nelly did not answer, and I exhaled a deep sigh of relief. I was not ready, not yet. Putting the phone aside, I turned back to my wardrobe, searching for something to calm my restless mind.

In my imagination, I saw myself stepping off the plane. The night air was cool, and a gentle breeze played with my long hair, tossing it in every direction as if whispering secrets of the journey ahead.

I walked toward the arrivals hall, the world around me alive with the festive spirit of Christmas. The airport buzzed with activity, a symphony of motion and sound. Passengers moved leisurely, scanning the conveyor belts for their luggage. Tiny children, cradled in their mothers' arms, slept peacefully, their dreams untouched by the commotion around them.

Everywhere I looked, ribbons of red and sparkling fairy lights adorned the space, casting a warm and magical glow. Airport staff wore cheerful Christmas hats, their smiles adding to the festive cheer. There was a collective energy in the air, a shared anticipation, as if everyone were standing at the threshold of a new beginning.

It felt as though the entire place moved in unison, bound together in a beautiful dance of harmony, carrying a sense of unity and joy. The colours, the lights, the energy everything blended perfectly, painting a scene of breathtaking beauty and infinite hope.

A tall man holding a placard with the word "Sunshine" written on it instantly drew my attention. A smile, unbidden and pure, spread across my face, rising from the depths of my heart. I began walking toward him, my excitement building with every step.

He seemed to recognize me too, his warm smile mirroring my own. As I approached, he extended his hand, his voice calm and welcoming as he said, "Welcome, Sunshine.

I shook his hand, my voice soft yet sincere. "Thank you for coming," I replied.

We shared a brief, knowing smile, and with a natural ease, he took my suitcase. Together, we walked out of the hall, stepping into the night as if the universe had orchestrated this very moment.

A sleek black Land Rover awaited us in the parking lot. The man courteously opened the door for me, and I slid into the back seat, settling in comfortably. He carefully placed my suitcase in the trunk, then climbed into the driver's seat and started the engine.

We had barely been on the road a few minutes when he broke the silence. I just realised I forgot to introduce myself, he said, glancing at me in the rearview mirror. "I am John, one of Chris's team members."

I smiled warmly and replied, "I am Anna, though Chris calls me Sunshine. It is a pleasure to meet you."

John returned the smile. "The pleasure is all mine," he said sincerely.

After a brief pause, he asked, "Is this your first time visiting New Zealand?"

"Yes," I answered.

"You are in for a treat," he said enthusiastically. "It is a stunning country with so many breathtaking places to explore. I hope you enjoy your stay."

"Thank you," I replied with a shy smile. "But honestly, I have come here only to see Chris."

John chuckled softly, a knowing glint in his eye. "Well then, I have no doubt you will have an amazing time."

We both laughed, the atmosphere in the car growing lighter as the conversation carried us forward. The gentle hum of the engine and the warm exchange of words made the moment feel like the beginning of something extraordinary.

The night was cloaked in darkness, yet amidst that stillness, nature glimmered under the soft, ethereal glow of the moonlight, painting a scene of quiet beauty.

John reached over and turned on the radio, and a gentle melody drifted through the car, weaving itself into the serenity of the night. The music made the journey feel even more magical, as if the universe had curated this moment just for me.

Curiosity got the better of me, and I could not help but ask how much longer it would take to reach our destination. It had been about 20 minutes since we began our drive.

"Do you know how much farther we must go?" I asked softly.

John, lowering the volume of the music just enough to hear me clearly, glanced in the rearview mirror and replied, "About 10 more minutes."

His calm voice blended perfectly with the music and the peaceful rhythm of the night, as if assuring me that the destination was worth the wait.

Before long, we found ourselves on a winding road that climbed steadily up a towering cliff. On one side, an endless forest stretched into the shadows, its canopy a dark, mysterious sea of leaves. On the other, the ocean roared with untamed power, its waves crashing against the rocks like the heartbeat of the earth itself.

It was a spellbinding dance of two magnificent worlds, each holding its own unfathomable secrets. Who could truly uncover the mysteries hidden in the depths of the ocean or the heart of the forest? These were ancient truths, whispered only between the sky and the earth, known to no one else.

Above it all, the moon draped its silvery veil over the scene, casting an otherworldly glow on land and sea alike. The wind sang softly, its melody weaving through the trees and across the waves, as if nature itself were composing a hymn to its own wonder. The beauty of the moment was both haunting and sublime, like a dream too perfect to be real.

At the end of the winding road, where the cliff met the sky, the soft glow of a house came into view, its golden lights cutting through the darkness like a beacon. As we drew closer to the grand entrance, the door opened seemingly on its own, as if the host had been anxiously awaiting my arrival, unable to contain their excitement any longer.

We stepped onto a beautifully crafted stone-paved pathway,

lined with neatly trimmed hedges and delicate lanterns that cast a soft, enchanting glow. The house ahead was nothing short of spectacular—a magnificent glass structure that seemed to merge seamlessly with the natural surroundings. Its walls, made almost entirely of glass, revealed glimpses of its glowing interior while framing the breathtaking panorama of the ocean on one side and the dense forest on the other. It felt like a sanctuary suspended between two worlds.

The light spilling from the house was warm and golden, illuminating the night with a quiet elegance. From the windows, the shimmer of soft chandeliers and the flicker of candles could be seen, casting playful shadows that danced across the walls.

At the front of the house, a short flight of wide stone steps led to a towering wooden door carved with intricate patterns that seemed to tell a story of their own. As I approached, the door swung open with a quiet grace, as though the house itself was inviting me in, whispering promises of comfort, wonder, and perhaps a little magic.

As the door opened, the silhouette of a man appeared, stepping onto the veranda at the top of the stairs. Slowly, he moved forward, each step deliberate, until he stopped at the edge, his presence commanding yet gentle. The car came to a quiet stop at the foot of the stairs, and there he stood, Chris.

His soft smile illuminated the night more than the stars

above, his gaze locked on mine with an intensity that held me captive. It was as if time itself had paused, waiting for this moment. John said something, but his words were lost to me, fading into the background like a forgotten melody.

I opened the door and stepped out, my heart beating in a rhythm only the night seemed to understand. I stood at the foot of the stairs, facing him. He extended his hand toward me, an unspoken invitation that carried the weight of a thousand unsaid words.

The wind, gentle and playful, caressed my hair as I ascended the stairs, one step at a time, drawn to him by an invisible force I could not resist. My eyes never left his, and his never left mine. Even in the velvety darkness, the brilliance of his blue eyes shone like twin stars, vivid and alive, as though the universe had poured its essence into them.

Above us, the sky was a grand chandelier, its countless stars glittering as if nature itself had prepared for this reunion. The waves crashed against the cliffs in a rhythmic symphony, their melody echoing through the night, while the wind's soft whisper added a tender harmony.

It felt as if the cosmos had conspired to create this moment, a celebration of love, unity, and divine orchestration. The universe, it seemed, had paused its eternal motion to light up the world for us, as though this meeting was its own masterpiece.

As his hand clasped mine, he said softly, his voice carrying the warmth of the night,

Chris: Welcome, Sunshine.

In that moment, I felt like a delicate flower, blooming at dawn on a spring morning—fresh, alive, and intoxicated with joy. I gently squeezed his hand and replied,

Me: I am so happy to see you, my blue sky.

Without another word, we embraced, and the world seemed to dissolve around us. Our hearts beat as one, their rhythm echoing in the stillness of the night. In that fleeting, perfect moment, there was nothing but us—no words, no barriers, just the quiet magic of being together.

The spell was broken by John's voice, pulling us gently back to reality.

John: Well, I will be heading off now. If you need anything, just give me a call. Oh, and I have already placed your suitcase in the room.

Chris and I both turned to thank him, our voices filled with gratitude, before he gave a courteous nod and disappeared into the night.

Chris turned back to me, his gaze filled with a quiet intensity, and said softly, "You have no idea how long I have waited for this moment. Seeing you now feels like a dream I never want to wake up from."

His words melted into the night, wrapping around me like the warmest embrace. I smiled, my heart racing as I replied, "And I feel like I am exactly where I was always meant to be with you."

The stars seemed to shine brighter, as if the universe itself celebrated the connection we shared.

His fingers, soft as silk, wove delicately through my hair, while the warmth of his breath brushed against my skin, sending shivers through my entire being. I felt as though we had stepped into another realm a world crafted solely for us, where everything existed in perfect harmony, untouched by the chaos of reality.

We were submerged in the depths of an endless ocean of kisses, the world around us fading away, when suddenly, a sound broke through the spell, pulling me back to myself.

I blinked, and in an instant, I was standing in front of the mirror in my room, a dress hanging limply in my hands. The name "Nelly" glowed brightly on my phone screen.

Oh no, Nelly. What am I going to say to her now? I thought, my mind racing as I reached for the phone.

I answered, trying to steady my voice.

Nelly: "Heeey, sis! How are you? What is new? I am so sorry I could not call earlier, I have been swamped today. Are you okay?

Her voice, as always, was bursting with energy, quick and animated. Nelly had this vibrant, unstoppable spirit, always filling the air with her enthusiasm, often sprinkled with playful mischief to make you laugh.

I replied softly, my tone steady and composed.

Me: Hi, darling. I am good, thank you. I just wanted to check in on you. How are you? How is the new job going?

Nelly: I am great, thanks! The new job is amazing, and the pay is fantastic!

Before I could say another word, she dove headfirst into a whirlwind of chatter, detailing her work and even venting about a few coworkers she did not like, calling them "jealous fools." Her words spilled out like a waterfall, her voice alive with her usual blend of humour and fire.

I stood there, listening, a small smile creeping onto my face. Nelly's energy was infectious, and even in moments like these, she managed to brighten my day with her relentless zest for life.

Before she could continue her endless chatter, I interrupted her.

Me: So, when are you coming back?

Nelly: I was planning to return next week, but I might stay a bit longer. One of the staff is going on vacation, and I am thinking of covering for them. But it is not confirmed yet.

Then, without missing a beat, she asked,

Nelly: "Why?"

I swallowed hard, my throat suddenly dry.

Me: I... I am seeing someone.

There was a pause before Nelly let out a series of small, excited squeals on the other end of the line, followed by loud laughter.

Nelly: Oh my God! Finally! You have found your soulmate! Tell me everything! Who is he? What does he look like? What does he do? Where is he from?

Her enthusiasm was infectious, and I could not help but laugh along with her. She was practically buzzing with excitement, firing off questions so quickly that I did not even have time to answer.

Me: If I tell you, you will not believe me.

Nelly: Come on, spill! Do you have a picture? Tell me everything!

Her rapid-fire questions came without pause, and it was clear she was more excited about this than I was. I laughed again, wondering how I would ever get a word in.

I finally mustered the courage to tell her everything and free myself of the weight I had been carrying. But just as I was about to speak, a voice called out her name from somewhere in the background.

"Hold on, I'll be right there!" Nelly called back, then quickly returned to our conversation.

Nelly: Alright, sis, I must go now, but you must tell me everything later! I want to know who this lucky guy is who managed to win over my sister's heart. Promise me, you will spill all the details when I call you back. Love you, kisses!

She did not even give me a chance to respond properly. As I scrambled for words, all I managed was, "Love you too, bye Nelly," before she hung up.

I lowered the phone, shaking my head with a small smile. Typical Nelly full of energy, leaving me with so much to say and no time to say it.

As I placed my phone on the bed, ready to return to my wardrobe, a message popped up.

Chris: Hey, Sunshine. I hope you are not missing me too much, followed by a heart and a smile emoji.

He continued, "I spoke with one of my staff members in London, someone I trust, and they mentioned that transferring money using a bank card could take a few days. But I want everything sorted out before I leave for London tomorrow. Have you ever sent money overseas? Do you know of a way to make the process faster?"

Seeing my new nickname on the screen filled me with excitement, and I quickly replied, "Of course, I miss you, adding a heart and kiss emoji."

I continued, "No, unfortunately, I have never sent money overseas before."

Chris: Alright, hang on a moment while I check something. I will get back to you shortly.

A few minutes later, another message popped up.

Chris: They told me the fastest way is through electronic money crypto. Do you have any crypto?

Feeling slightly flustered, I responded, I know what it is, but no, I do not have any.

Chris: No problem. You can buy Bitcoin with just $500 and send it. That way, the money will reach the office in London instantly.

I had no clue what it was; I had only heard the name mentioned a few times by Nelly and in passing conversations about her deals.

Nelly seemed to know a lot about these things. I knew she had made some good money buying and selling them before, and she had even shared a small part of her profit with me.

Still, I did not feel like asking her.

Me: Okay, so how do I buy it and send it?

Chris, clearly in a hurry, responded almost immediately, "You need a crypto app. Do you have one?"

Me: No, I do not. I do not even know which app I am supposed to use.

He quickly sent me the names of a few apps and, at the end of the list, pointed out one specifically, "This one is the best."

Then he followed it up with an address, something that looked vaguely like an email but strange and unfamiliar to me.

Chris: Buy Bitcoin with the money and send it to this address.

I felt the usual wave of anxiety that always hit me when I faced something completely new and unknown. Struggling to keep my composure, I said:

Me: Alright, I will download it first.

I started downloading the app and entering my details.

Chris, clearly impatient, messaged again, "Let me know how far you have gotten."

Me: I just finished downloading it.

He immediately began guiding me step by step, explaining which options to select, how to make the purchase, and how to send it. Whenever I ran into a problem, he would ask me to take a screenshot and send it to him so he could explain more clearly. I followed his instructions exactly.

But no matter what I did, the app would not let me make the purchase. Frustrated, I ended up downloading several other apps, but none of them worked either. It was incredibly strange.

Life had taught me one thing, whenever something does not work out without a clear reason, it is a sign to walk away. This belief had never failed me. Yet, I could not bring myself to tell Chris.

To be honest, that day turned out to be the longest conversation we had ever had, all focused on this money transfer.

And amidst all the instructions and troubleshooting, Chris kept saying things like, "Sunshine, my dear, it makes me so happy to see you trying so hard to make this happen for us."

Those sweet little compliments filled me with hope and made me even more determined to succeed.

AND HE KEPT REPEATING, DO NOT RUSH, MY DEAR. TAKE YOUR TIME.

The sky was almost dark, and my phone battery had died several times. I kept trying over and over, but nothing worked. Completely exhausted and on the verge of giving up, my phone rang, it was Nelly. I knew I had to answer. She was probably bursting with excitement and dying to hear all the details.

I picked up, and before I could say a word, Nelly's voice bubbled over with energy.

Nelly: Hey, sis! I just finished work, and I am heading home. So… tell me everything! Where did you two meet?

She squealed with delight, her excitement practically radiating through the phone.

"Oh my God, I am so happy for you!" she added.

I could not help but smile at her enthusiasm and replied, "We have not met yet… but I know him."

Nelly: What? Does that mean I know him too? Alright, who is it?

Me: His name is Chris.

Nelly: Chris? Chris?

She repeated the name several times, trying to figure it out.

"Which Chris? I really cannot remember!" she said, sounding completely puzzled.

My throat felt dry, and my face was damp with sweat as I finally blurted out:

Me: Chris Martin.

Nelly still did not seem to get it.

Nelly: "Chris Martin? Is he an old friend of yours? I do not remember anyone by that name. Come on, just tell me who he is!"

Swallowing nervously, I tried to explain, but before I could finish, she burst out laughing.

Nelly: Shut up! Are you kidding me? You are pulling my leg, aren't you?

She laughed so hard I could hear the disbelief in her voice.

Me: I am serious! Wait, let me send you, his pictures.

I quickly started sending her the photos Chris had sent me.

As she looked at them, she said:

Nelly: These? These are the same kinds of pictures you can find all over the internet. Are you seriously trying to convince me, or is this a joke? You are such an idiot!

She laughed so much that she claimed tears were streaming down her face.

Determined, I started telling her the entire story from the beginning. She kept interrupting, laughing, and asking questions.

Then, she asked me to send her the video messages Chris had sent, but I explained that they disappeared after each viewing.

Nelly: Alright, sis. I still do not believe any of this, but there is no way I am letting you go to New Zealand alone. You will have to wait because I am coming with you.

Her words shocked me, and I quickly replied, "No, you cannot come! I promised him I would not tell anyone."

Nelly: There is no way I am letting you go alone.

Then, after a pause, she said, "Honestly, I do not think any of this is real."

Me: What about the videos and voice messages? That is his voice! Those videos were of Chris himself, talking to me, calling my name!

Nelly: My dear, sweet sister, why are you so trusting? What if it is a fraud?

Her words hit me like a bucket of ice-cold water poured over my head. I froze, whispering to myself,

A fraud? A fraud? How could it possibly be a fraud?

Nelly, hearing my murmured disbelief, gently said, "You had not even thought of that, had you?" Then, her voice softened with concern, Oh, Anna, my darling.

Sensing the panic building inside me, she quickly tried to ease the tension,

Nelly: But hey, maybe you are right. Maybe it is him.

Her tone grew calmer, more thoughtful as if she realised how deeply her words had shaken me.

Nelly: Listen, sis, I will be back next week. Until then, promise me you will not go anywhere, and keep me updated every day on what is going on between you two. Anna, you know how much I love you, right?

I felt paralysed by fear and doubt, the weight of her words pressing down on me. My voice barely came out as I said,

Me: I love you too, Nelly.

After a moment of hesitation, I asked quietly,

Me: Do you think someone could look and sound so much like Chris just to deceive me?

Nelly paused for a moment, as though choosing her words carefully, before replying,

Nelly: It is possible… but not highly likely. Still, there are apps now technology that can mimic someone's face and voice almost perfectly. If someone wanted to trick you, they could pull it off.

Her words lingered in the air like a storm cloud, leaving me with a heavy, unshakable sense of unease.

Chapter 7

A Shattered Reality

Despite Nelly's words and the harsh reality laid bare by countless articles, a part of me clung to the belief that it was Chris. The heart has its reasons, of which reason knows nothing, I reminded myself. How could the connection I felt, so profound and resonant, be entirely false? Could a scammer truly fabricate not just the appearance and voice but the very essence of someone I admired so deeply?

As these thoughts swirled in my mind, I found myself defending the belief to Nelly, my voice was a mix of defiance and desperation.

Me: "But Nelly, everything he said, the way he understood my thoughts, my dreams… it was so real. How could all of that be just an act?"

Nelly listened, her expression a blend of sympathy and concern. After a pause, she spoke softly,

Nelly: "Anna, sometimes, we see what we want to see. But holding onto hope is not wrong. Just… be cautious."

That night, I could not bring myself to dismantle the last bastions of my belief. Not yet. I needed more proof, something undeniable, to sever what my heart still held onto. So, I decided to keep these revelations to myself a little longer, to observe and search for the undeniable truth that would finally persuade my heart to let go, or to hold on to the wondrous possibility that it was all real, after all.

On one side, doubts, and Nelly's words—a sister whom I had trusted my entire life—were eating away at me, and on the other, the sweetness of those beautiful moments I had created with Chris in my world had left me bewildered and dazed.

I decided to reach out to Chris with a message filled with longing.

Me: "Hello, my blue sky. I have missed you. Can you send me a picture of yourself, just to keep my heart at ease?"

I waited anxiously, watching as the hours ticked by slowly, my phone remaining hauntingly silent. As the night deepened, the lack of response weighed heavily on me, stirring a restless sense of foreboding.

I returned to the YouTube page where I had originally commented, my fingers trembling as I scrolled through the sea of words. My heart beat a frantic rhythm, each thump a silent prayer, hoping against hope not to unearth any truth that might shatter my fragile belief.

As I read, each comment unfolded benignly; there was nothing amiss. Relief washed over me like a gentle wave, and I allowed my eyes to close, surrendering to a moment of peace.

In that serene solitude, I envisioned myself draped in an ethereal gown of white lace, adorned with voluminous flowers embossed with intricate patterns, and sleeves that billowed like soft clouds. My long, wavy hair cascaded over my shoulders, a waterfall of soft curls. I stood holding a glass of deep red wine, my gaze fixed through the panoramic glass walls of an airy, crystalline house, mesmerized by the moon's silvery light dancing on the boundless ocean.

Suddenly, the soft hum of music filled the air, its melody tender and inviting. It was "Dance with Me", a song woven with nostalgia and longing. Turning slowly, I found Chris standing there, his hand outstretched toward me, a gentle smile gracing his lips.

"Tonight, it's just you and me," he said softly. "Let's make this moment last forever."

Placing the glass of wine aside, I took his hand, and he drew me close. His other arm wrapped around my waist with a natural grace, pulling me into him as though we had always been meant to fit together. We began to sway, our steps light and unhurried, the music guiding our movements like a gentle tide.

"Why this song?" I asked, my voice barely louder than a whisper, my gaze locked on his.

"Because it reminds me of the night, I knew you were my forever," he replied, his tone warm and filled with certainty. "You've always been my dream, my poem, my melody."

A smile curved my lips, and he twirled me with effortless elegance, our laughter mingling with the soft notes of the music. As the song swelled, our steps slowed, the world around us fading into nothing but the rhythm of our hearts and the warmth of his embrace.

With a tender touch, he rested his forehead against mine, his breath mingling with mine as he whispered, "Every moment with you is a gift."

I wrapped my arms around his neck, my voice trembling with emotion. "You complete me. I never want this moment to end."

O sacred rain, oh love divine,

Upon my thirsty soul, now shine.

With drops of passion, pure and deep,

Embrace me soft, let longing weep.

Fall like whispers, warm and sweet,

A tender kiss where night and dreams meet.

Till barren fields in bloom arise,

Beneath your touch, like paradise.

The song faded, leaving behind a serene silence that wrapped around us like a gentle veil. Yet, neither of us moved away. The moon's silvery light bathed us, its glow reflecting off the glass walls and casting soft shadows that seemed to dance with us.

Chris's hand brushed my cheek as he tilted my face toward him, his lips were a mere whisper away. "Now, it is just you and me. Nothing else matters."

Our embrace deepened, crafting a breathtaking tableau under the celestial dance of the moon and the expansive sky. Together, we wove moments of profound unity that stretched into dawn, a blissful blend of love and delight, a seamless merging of one soul into two bodies. I surrendered my heart and soul to him, wishing never to break from this dream, yearning to stay forever cradled in this sublime slumber.

The sound of something falling from a height shattered my sweet world and woke me up. It was Kitty. Sometimes, at night, like a tireless mischief-maker, she would knock over whatever was on the table or any high place.

With a tone of fatigue mixed with a faint smile, I said, "Oh, Kitty… this isn't the time for that."

But my heart was beating faster, a strange warmth had enveloped my entire being, and a peculiar feeling, like losing something precious, was flowing through me. I whispered under my breath:

"I wish I had never woken up… I wish I could stay in that dream forever."

I lay on the bed, my gaze fixed on the sky visible through my window. The stars shone like luminous points of hope in the sea of darkness. I took a deep breath and softly said:

The night is beautiful because it is lit by your stars.

The moon is beautiful because it glows in the radiance of your gaze.

The cloud is beautiful because it overflows with your freshness.

The sky is beautiful because it has taken on the boundlessness of your infinity.

The ocean is beautiful because its calm comes from the depth of your silence.

And love is beautiful because it carries the eternal warmth of you within itself.

And I… I learned to love with you.

In your world, I experienced flight in every form I ever dreamed of, without fear or restraint.

You were a land that freed me from the bounds of every limit.

With you, my nights were illuminated, and my days were filled with the scent of eternity.

But now… now, only Kitty's noise stays, and I am left alone in this void, living only with the memory of your dream.

But now, awakened by Kitty's noise from a sweet dream, I opened my eyes to sunlight streaming through the window, and everything was calm and quiet. I sat up, recalling the moments, a dream so vivid I could hardly believe that it was just a dream. Your image was still etched in my mind, those kind smiles and deep looks that shook my heart every time. In that dream, I danced with you in that dreamland and experienced love.

Now, I got up and walked to the window. Kitty sat by my side, looking outside. I felt lonely, but at the same time, the memory of your presence in that dream gave me the strength to start my day. With every step, I tried to apply the lessons learned in that dream world and move forward in my life with hope for better days.

I quickly went to check my phone, but I had not received any messages from him yet. Initially, I was a bit worried, then I went on Instagram to see if there was any new update from him, but I found nothing that could calm me down. I told myself he must be busy or in the middle of performing and rehearsing their program. I tried to convince myself.

I sent him a message:

Me: "Good morning, my blue sky, I hope you have a very beautiful day."

I waited a moment, but there was no response, then I sent him a beautiful song by Cyril, "Stumblin' In."

Let me know if this meets your needs or if there is anything else you would like to adjust!

As always, I turned on the music and tackled the backlog of tasks, hoping to divert my mind from the wait. There were many things I had not managed to address in the past few days.

Then, I composed this verse for him:

Fall, oh sanctifying rain of existence,

Anoint this dried husk, weary and worn.

Pour forth your rain of love and compassion,

That my barren field of waiting might flourish once more.

The sun was positioned directly mid-sky, marking the passage of half the day, yet there was still no news. Growing gradually anxious, I checked all the band's social media pages, but everything appeared normal—only a few old photos and songs had been posted.

Deciding I needed a distraction, I opted to go to the shopping centre, hoping it would make time pass a little quicker. I slipped on a simple t-shirt, jeans, and sports shoes, got into my car, and drove to the mall. Although our house is very close to the shopping centre, I always prefer to drive. Contrary to many women, I really do not enjoy shopping and would rather quickly grab what I need and head back home.

I parked as close as possible to the entrance and quickly headed upstairs to the food stores. I picked up a trolley and swiftly shopped for the items I needed. Throughout my shopping, I checked my phone several times but still, there was no news.

I bumped into a few friends and acquaintances, and quickly exchanged greetings, showing that I was in a hurry and not in the mood for chatting. As I was heading back to my car, my phone rang.

It was Nelly. After the usual pleasantries, she wanted to check in, probably worried about me. I reassured her that everything was fine and that I would not do anything without letting her know. She then asked me to stop by the post office to pick up a parcel that had arrived for her.

I put the items in the car and went back upstairs. The post office was on the ground floor, and just before it, there was a large jewellery store displaying dazzling, expensive pieces. I stopped for a moment, my eyes drawn to the sparkling rings, necklaces, and earrings behind the glass, each more enchanting than the last.

As I gazed at the jewels, I suddenly saw myself inside the store, but I was not alone. Chris was there with me, holding my hand, his touch warm and reassuring. He leaned in close, whispering something in my ear that made me laugh. We stood together, carefree and smiling, surrounded by the brilliance of the jewels, as if the entire store were aglow just for us.

The salesperson presented us with an array of exquisite rings, each adorned with vibrant, colourful gemstones. I tried them on one by one, marvelling at the unique charm of each piece.

Amidst all the dazzling options, one ring captured my attention, a delicate creation with several small, shimmering stones, in silvery tones, elegantly set in white gold. It radiated a quiet beauty that stood out from the rest, drawing me in completely.

I gently slipped the ring onto my finger, admiring how perfectly it fit. Placing my hand over my heart, I gazed at my reflection in the mirror. The white gold seemed to come alive, shimmering softly against my skin, as if it were meant to belong to me.

Chris, standing beside me, smiled, and said, "It's absolutely beautiful, and it suits you perfectly." His words, warm and sincere, made the moment feel even more special.

I turned to the salesperson and, with a smile, requested an engraving on the inside of the ring. I wanted it to carry something meaningful, something that would always remind me of this moment. "Please engrave 'BS – Blue Sky and Sunshine, I said, imagining the words etched forever on this delicate piece of art.

I was still lost in the moment when the sound of a message notification pulled me back to reality.

It was from Chris. My heart skipped a beat as I quickly opened a voice message.

Chris's familiar, warm voice filled the air, "Hello, my sunshine. I have missed you so much. I am sorry for being so busy, but not a single moment has gone by without you on my mind."

His words lingered, wrapping around me like a gentle embrace, making the world around me feel brighter.

Hearing his voice, something deep within me melted—a feeling so indescribable, like a golden light cascading through me, wrapping every corner of my being in warmth and serenity. It was as if his words had the power to touch my very soul.

I wanted to respond with a voice message, to let him hear the emotions his words had stirred, but my voice was trembling too much to speak. Instead, I chose to write, pouring my heart into every word.

Me: Hello, Blue Sky. I have missed you more than words can express. I know how busy you are, and I understand, but I cannot help wishing I were by your side, sharing even a small part of your world.

I hesitated for a moment before hitting send, wondering if my words truly captured everything I felt, but in the end, I knew they carried the truth of my heart.

I put the phone in my pocket and quickly headed to the post office. Once I finished my task, I got into the car and drove back home. The streets were busy, and soft music was playing on the radio, but my mind was still occupied with the messages I had exchanged with Chris.

When I got home, I felt a little tired, but an invisible excitement was coursing through me. The ring I had imagined buying felt as though it was already on my finger. I had not bought it yet, but in my mind, every detail had taken shape, the shimmer of the stones, the smoothness of the white gold, and the words I envisioned engraved on it, etched into my heart.

A few minutes later, my phone buzzed again. It was another message from Chris. I took a deep breath, picked up the phone, and opened it.

His warm and familiar voice sounded softer and closer this time, "I wish you were here with me too. My world feels incomplete without you."

His voice felt like a whisper in my ear, stopping everything around me. A pure and deep feeling coursed through me, as if his words were a golden light passing through me, filling every corner of my heart with unparalleled warmth and serenity.

I wanted to write something back, but the words had escaped my mind. I just imagined holding that ring in my hand, thinking of the words engraved on it: BS – Blue Sky and Sunshine.

I told myself that maybe life, with all its complexities, is sometimes simpler than we think. Maybe, sometimes, we just need to trust the flow of emotions, even if it does not seem logical.

But amidst the magic of the moment, something unsettled me. An unknown feeling, like a distant whisper, seemed to want to reveal a truth that I could not fully grasp yet. This feeling was like a small crack in the middle of my dreams, slowly starting to widen.

He then sent me a photo of himself, his familiar smile lighting up his face as always. Moments later, he asked me to send him a picture in return.

Without a second thought, I sent him one.

It felt as if I had known him my entire life, as though he had always been a part of my world.

I asked him when he would be returning, and he replied that he was not sure yet but promised to let me know as soon as he had more information.

I was waiting for him to mention the membership card, but he did not say a word about it. Gathering my courage, I decided to ask, "By the way, did you receive the membership card?"

There was a brief pause before he replied.

Chris: Oh, I am so sorry, I completely forgot. I have been so busy. I had asked one of my staff to handle it, and they said it would be best if you sent the money via PayPal.

Then he added, "Hold on, let me get the PayPal address for you, and I'll let you know."

After a few minutes, he sent me an email address and instructed me to send the money to that account through PayPal.

Blinded by my eagerness to connect with him, I quickly responded, "Of course."

He then asked me to send him the receipt, once I made the payment. I followed his instructions without hesitation, as though I were under a spell. Like a loyal servant, I carried out his every command without question, completely captivated by the thought of being closer to him.

I was about to open the PayPal app when a call from Nelly interrupted me, stopping me mid-task. She probably wanted to check if I had received the package.

Me: "Hi, Nelly. I got the package."

Nelly: Hey, sis! Oh, you sound like you are in such a rush. Is everything okay?

She could sense the urgency in my voice. I smiled and replied, "No, nothing. I just forgot to text you earlier to let you know I received it.

Nelly: Thanks, love. Now, tell me—what has got you so rushed? And by the way, she added with a teasing tone, how is your new love?

Her question made my heart race. I was scared to tell her; afraid she would try to stop me. Keeping it brief, I explained that he had been messaging me and was currently in London.

Nelly: You know, last night I was scrolling through Instagram and saw so many stories about online scams. I thought I should warn you to be careful.

Then, with a gentler voice, she asked, have you done any research about him? Are you sure it is him?

For a moment, my hands began to tremble, and an overwhelming sense of fear gripped me. It felt as though the world around me had gone dark. I took a deep breath, trying to shake it off, and said, "Well, I have heard his voice, and he sends me videos and talks to me. Could it be fake?

Nelly paused before responding, "Anna, I know you have a beautiful, trusting heart. That is one of the things I love most about you. But in today's world, anything is possible. Technology allows people to do things we could not even imagine."

Just then, my phone buzzed with a message from Chris.

"Okay, I will look into it more, told Nelly quickly before saying goodbye and hanging up."

Chris: I have arranged a beautiful and special place for you. I want you to be there before I return, my sunshine. He added a heart and a smiling emoji.

His words completely swept me off my feet, making me forget everything Nelly had warned me about. Without a second thought, I transferred the money, took a picture of the receipt, and sent it to him.

Me: I am counting down the moments until I can see you, my blue sky. Even though, you are already with me in every part of my soul. I added a heart and a kiss emoji, pouring all my emotions into the message.

Then I added, "By the way, I have sent the money, and here is the receipt for it."

It took him a little while to reply, but when he did, he said, "Thank you, my love. I will let you know as soon as I hear anything. Take care of yourself, my dearest."

I placed my phone aside, trying to catch my breath, but another notification popped up almost instantly, it was Nelly. She had sent me a few posts.

With trembling hands, I opened them one by one. Each word, each warning on the screen made my heart pound harder, the sound echoing in the silent house like a relentless drumbeat. My knees buckled, and I sank to the floor, the weight of an unspoken fear pressing down on me. My breaths came in short, sharp gasps as if the very air around me had thickened.

I forced myself to open the page where I had left that fateful comment. My vision blurred as I scrolled through the comments. Messages from strangers beneath the band's posts screamed warnings: "Watch out for scams. Do not trust anyone. Never click on suspicious links."

The words burned into my mind. My world began to collapse in on itself, like a house of cards blown apart by a harsh wind. Darkness crept in, swallowing every trace of hope. It felt as though the ground beneath me had vanished, leaving me in a freefall with no end in sight.

Like a frantic, desperate soul, I spiraled through the cold expanse of the internet, my mind racing as I searched for answers. Every thought, no matter how irrational, I typed into the search bar, whispering under my breath, "It has to be a mistake. It must be! Maybe it's a scam for others, but not for me. Not for me!"

My hands trembled as I scrolled, my eyes darting across the room, yet I saw nothing but fragmented memories of those fleeting, blissful moments. His voice, his words—they echoed in my mind like distant whispers, teasing me with their familiarity.

I opened our messages with trembling fingers, replaying

every voice note. Each one felt so real, so vivid. His tone, the pauses, the warmth, it was him. It had to be him.

But no matter how many times I listened; an unsettling doubt began to creep into the edges of my mind. My breaths grew shallow, and my chest tightened. I clung to my phone as if it held the truth, the lifeline to my unravelling reality.

I took a deep, shaky breath, but it only made the anxiety worse. My throat burned with thirst, and I grabbed a glass of water, gulping it down as if I could drown the rising panic. But even as I poured a second glass, the dryness inside me remained, a suffocating, unquenchable emptiness.

The room spun around me, and I clung to the only thing that felt real: his words. But even they began to blur, slipping through my grasp like sand in an hourglass. Could it all have been a lie? No. It could not be. It cannot be.

Memories of the hardest days of my life came rushing back, the day I lost my mother, and years later, my father, my greatest supporter, and dearest friend. The pain of those moments lingered, woven into the fabric of who I was.

Tears began to spill from my eyes, unstoppable, even though I had not permitted them to fall. It was as if my heart had taken over, releasing all the emotions I was too afraid to confront.

I could not tell if I was trapped in a terrible nightmare or floating in a beautiful, fragile dream. My mind was spinning, caught in a whirlwind of disbelief, sorrow, and longing, leaving me lost and utterly adrift.

I sat there, frozen, clutching my phone as if it were the only anchor to a world that suddenly felt unfamiliar. My mind refused to rest, spiraling with questions I could not answer. What if I was wrong? What if all of this, his words, his voice, his promises—was nothing more than a beautifully crafted illusion?

I replayed one of the voice notes again, closing my eyes as his words filled the room. It was him, wasn't it? The way he spoke, the pauses between his sentences, the warmth in his tone—it had to be him. But a quiet voice in the back of my mind refused to be silenced: What if it is not?

The thought hit me like a punch to the chest, stealing the air from my lungs. I stood up abruptly, pacing the room as if movement might somehow quiet the storm within me. But the storm grew louder, relentless, each step fueling the chaos inside. I whispered to myself, as though clinging to a fragile lifeline, "It is real. It must be real."

My hands trembled as I grabbed my phone, scrolling through our messages with desperate urgency. My eyes landed on one in particular, "Take care of yourself, my sunshine." Those words had once wrapped around me like a warm hug, but now they felt distant, like an echo from a place I could no longer reach.

A memory surfaced unbidden, cutting through my thoughts like a shard of light, my father's voice, steady and unwavering, "Always trust your instincts, but never ignore the signs." His words lingered, heavy with meaning, as though he were standing beside me now, urging me to see what I did not want to face.

But I did not want to face it. Not yet.

I sank back into the chair, my phone still clutched tightly in my hand. The room felt suffocatingly quiet, the silence pressing in on me until it became deafening. I reached for the glass of water on the table, draining it in one gulp, but the hollow ache in my chest remained. No amount of water could quench the parched, suffocating void inside me.

My heart and mind were locked in a battle I could not escape, one grasping desperately at the hope that this was real, the other pulling me toward the cracks forming in the illusion I had so carefully constructed.

Then, the phone buzzed in my hand, shattering the stillness like a sudden clap of thunder. My breath caught as I opened the message.

"Hey, sunshine. Just checking in. Did you get a chance to send it?"

The words were simple, casual even, but they struck me differently now. My fingers hovered over the keyboard, frozen. I wanted to respond the way I always had—with warmth, excitement, and trust, but something had shifted.

For the first time, I wasn't sure if I was replying to a dream or stepping deeper into a lie.

I took a deep, shaky breath, my mind racing. Then a chilling realization hit me—I had already sent him the receipt. My stomach twisted as I scrolled back to confirm it, the message glaring back at me like an accusation. My hands moved on their own, resending it again, as though the act might quiet the doubts gnawing at my mind.

I waited, my eyes fixed on the screen, my heart pounding with every second that passed. The familiar typing indicator appeared, then vanished, then reappeared, as if even his words hesitated.

Finally, the reply came, "Thanks, sunshine. I appreciate it. Things are just so hectic right now with the charity event. You're my calm in the storm."

The words were perfect, so perfect they felt rehearsed. I read them again and again, searching for something, anything, to reassure me. But instead, they only deepened the ache inside me.

My father's voice echoed once more: "Trust your instincts."

I stood up again, unable to sit still, my breath shallow and uneven. My mind replayed every interaction, every word. How had I ignored the little signs? The deflected questions, the unmet promises, the carefully constructed phrases that always seemed to soothe without revealing anything real.

Tears burned at the corners of my eyes, but I refused to let them fall. Instead, I stared out the window, the city lights blurring into a haze. The truth I had been running from was no longer a distant possibility, it was here, staring back at me.

And yet, even now, I wanted to believe. I wanted so desperately to believe.

Me: Chris, can you send me a video of yourself? While you are talking, could you run your hand through your hair? It is just something small, but it would mean a lot to me.

Chris said with a pause, "Sunshine, why are you asking this? You know I am not the kind of person who has time to record random videos. My schedule is crazy right now with the charity event, the meetings, the travel plans. It is just… not possible."

Me: I understand you are busy, but it would only take a minute. I am not asking for much, Chris. I just need to see you.

Chris: See me? You have already seen everything you need to. Haven't I proven myself to you by now? Why would you doubt me like this?

Me: I do not doubt you, Chris. It is not about doubt; it is about reassurance. You mean so much to me, and I just need this small thing to put my mind at ease.

Chris: (Slightly irritated) Sunshine, you are hurting me right now. I have shared so much with you—my time, my trust, my dreams. And now you are questioning me over something so trivial?

Me: It is not trivial to me. Please, Chris. I would not ask if it were not important.

Chris: Important? Do you think this is important when I have a million things on my plate? Do you even understand the kind of pressure I am under? My entire day is planned down to the minute. I cannot just stop everything for this.

Me: Chris, it is just one minute. You could do it right now and be done with it. If you care about how I feel, if you care about us, you will do this for me.

Chris said with a long pause, "Sunshine, I do not even know what to say. Your lack of trust… is breaking my heart. But fine. If this is what it takes, then I will do it. I hope you realise what you are asking me for."

Me: Thank you, Chris. I did not mean to hurt you. I just need to see you—to feel close to you.

(After several minutes, a video arrives. In it, Chris appears calm but visibly frustrated.)

Chris (in the video): Sunshine, this is hard for me. I have given you everything, but it seems like it is not enough. You have hurt me by doubting me, but I am doing this because I care about you.

(He runs his hand through his hair as he speaks, just as you asked, his tone firm yet tender.)

Chris (in the video): I hope this clears your doubts because I do not know if I can take much more of this. Trust is everything, Sunshine. Without it, what do we even have?

(Back to the messages)

Me: Chris, I am sorry. I did not mean to make you feel like this. I just… I needed to know.

Chris: I am trying, Sunshine. But you have made me feel like I am not enough for you. After everything, this is what you think of me?

I knew the video would disappear after one viewing, so before opening it, I used my phone to record it directly from the screen of my laptop. This way, I would have it saved in my gallery, something tangible to hold onto.

Afterward, I watched it over and over again. It was him, sitting in the corner of a room, speaking to me. His voice, his gestures—everything seemed right.

For a moment, I felt a sense of relief. But deep down, a small part of me still needed validation. I wanted someone else to see it, to confirm that I was not just imagining things.

I sent the video to Nelly, my closest confidant, along with an explanation of everything that had happened between Chris and me. I told her about the messages, the promises, the doubts, and how I had asked him for the video to ease my mind.

As I waited for her response, my heart raced. I was not sure what I wanted her to say. Perhaps, I just needed someone to tell me that I was right, that my dream was not unravelling before my eyes.

That night, for the first time in what felt like ages, I felt peace settle over me like a soft blanket, and I closed my eyes.

The room buzzed with life and energy. Chris and the rest of the band were immersed in their final preparations, their focus and excitement almost palpable. I stood quietly in the corner of the makeup room, unnoticed but completely captivated, my heart swelling with a mix of admiration and joy.

I knew they were about to create something magical, a performance that would explode with love and joy, igniting a connection with their fans that was as powerful as it was mutual. The air itself seemed to hum with anticipation, charged with an unspoken bond between the band and the audience awaiting them.

It was a night destined to be unforgettable, overflowing with energy, passion, and a love so profound it felt like it could light up the world.

Everyone was ready. The energy in the room was electric, a

quiet buzz of anticipation filling the air. Chris walked toward me with calm confidence, his eyes locked on mine, as though the world around us had disappeared.

He pulled me into his arms, holding me close, and leaned in until his face was just inches from mine. I could feel the warmth of his breath against my skin, a quiet reassurance in the chaos of the moment.

With a playful smile, I said softly, "Well, my golden-throated swallow, they're all waiting to see which love song you've brought to life for them tonight."

His lips curved into a gentle smile, his eyes filled with something unspoken, a mix of gratitude and love. "Tonight's song will be my best," he murmured, his voice low but steady. "Because Sunshine is here with me."

His words wrapped around my heart like a melody, and before I could respond, he leaned in, and our lips met. The kiss was brief, yet it carried the weight of a thousand promises.

As he pulled away, his hand lingered on mine for a moment longer. "Wish me luck," he whispered, his voice like a secret meant only for me.

"You don't need it," I replied with a quiet laugh. "You've already won them over."

He smiled again, his expression lighter now, before turning

and joining the others. I watched as they walked toward the stage, the hum of the crowd growing louder in the distance. And in that moment, I knew he was not just singing for them, he was singing for me, too.

Like every morning, I woke up to the gentle nudge of Kitty, her soft paws brushing against me.

I murmured, "Hey, Kitty… if only you knew where I have been. If only you had not woken me up." My voice was heavy as if I were speaking to myself as much as to her.

Instinctively, I reached for my phone, my heart leaping for a moment, only to sink again. No messages from Chris.

Instead, there were several notifications from Nelly.

Before opening them, I quickly typed a message to Chris:

"Good morning, my blue sky. I hope you have a beautiful day." I added a few heart emojis, hoping to hide the unease that had crept into my chest.

I hesitated for a moment, then opened Nelly's messages. One of them was a video. My curiosity turned to dread as I clicked play.

The moment the video started; I froze. My hands began to tremble, and my breath caught in my throat. It felt as though the ground beneath me had disappeared, leaving me suspended in a void.

I watched the video again. And again. Each replay drove the dagger deeper into my heart.

It was him. Chris.

My heart pounded painfully in my chest as if it could shatter at any moment. Tears poured down my face, unstoppable, relentless, like a storm breaking over a fragile shore.

The video was undeniable. The man I thought I knew, the man I had trusted with my dreams, was staring back at me, but not as the person I believed him to be.

The world around me blurred, reduced to the sound of my ragged breathing and the thudding of my heart. At that moment, everything I thought was real began to crumble.

And she added, "My dear, I know this is hard for you to accept, but as I have told you before, with the advancements in technology today, anything can be faked. People can create whatever they want, and it can seem so real. Please, do not let this break you. If you ever want to talk, I am here. Just call me anytime. I love you, sis."

She added a string of heart and kiss emojis, her warmth radiating even through the screen.

The video was the same as the one sent to me—same place, same clothes, and the same gesture of him running his hand through his hair, except this time, he was addressing his fans.

My God. I froze on the spot, paralysed by the weight of realisation. A hollow emptiness consumed me, and the world around me blurred into shadows. My body trembled violently as if it could barely contain the storm brewing inside.

All those days, those precious moments, every honeyed word he spoke, words that had felt like the sweetest nectar, now turned into venom, poisoning every part of me. It felt as though the sky itself was raining fire, and my tears burned as they streamed down my face. Gravity abandoned me, and for a moment, I crumbled to the ground, overwhelmed by the eruption of pain and betrayal within me.

I lay there, lost in the searing chaos of my emotions, unable to escape the molten waves of despair that engulfed my soul.

My body refused to acknowledge the existence of my soul. The pain was overwhelming, sharp yet untraceable, coursing through me so intensely that even breathing became a struggle.

My ears seemed deaf to the world, catching only faint, haunting murmurs from some distant, unreachable place. My eyes, blinded by despair, could see nothing but an inferno of flames and a swirling black storm, raging with a force that annihilated everything in its path.

I was helpless, trapped in the eye of this merciless tempest, a force so destructive it left no part of me untouched. It consumed everything, my thoughts, my strength, my hope, leaving behind only emptiness and ashes.

That night, I wandered through a void of numbness and shock, disconnected from the world as if I no longer belonged to it. The colour of the sky escaped me; the sun was nothing more than a forgotten memory.

I could not comprehend what had happened to me. It was as if I had stood on the edge of the apocalypse, watching the world collapse into ruin while I remained, a broken fragment amidst the chaos.

Was I awake, or trapped in a dream I could not escape? I did not know. Time became an endless abyss—seconds stretched into hours; hours blurred into years. Every moment felt eternal, yet insubstantial, as though I was caught in the void between existence and oblivion.

Chapter 8

Lessons of the Heart

The next morning, as I opened my eyes, I felt like a completely different person, as if the old me had been left behind in the wreckage of the night before.

I picked up my phone and saw a few messages from Nelly and two from "Chris."

This time, I replied to Nelly first. I wrote that I was fine, that she should not worry about me, and that I was just a bit busy. I promised to call her when the time was right. I did not want to worry her, so I pretended I was okay, even though, deep down, I knew she would not believe it.

Then, I turned to the messages from the person pretending to be Chris. My hands trembled, but this time, it was not from sorrow. It was fury, raw, seething rage, mixed with an overwhelming sense of disgust.

In my mind, I tried to name him, to give form to the loathing I felt. A scavenger? No. A hyena? No. Nothing seemed right, until finally, one word surfaced: Plague.

That is what he was...a disease, spreading destruction, leaving ruin wherever he went.

I stared at his messages, my jaw tightening. This time, I was not going to let him win.

Plague: "Hello, my dear sunshine. I have missed you so much. Send me a new picture so I can see my beautiful sun and feel energized. I cannot wait to see you."

Attached to the message was a photo of him, smiling with a confidence that made my stomach churn. His eyes mocked me as if he truly believed he still had me under his spell.

The words, the photo, everything about the message was a spark to the inferno already raging inside me. Anger, humiliation, and disgust swirled together, suffocating me.

Without hesitation, I opened my gallery and began removing every single photo and video I had ever sent him. With each deletion, I felt a mixture of relief and agony, as if I were clawing out pieces of my soul.

"Idiot. Fool. How could you fall for this? You are so naive. So blind," I whispered to myself, the accusations tumbling out faster than my tears.

Tears poured down my face in hot, uncontrollable streams, blurring my vision as I continued. My fingers moved furiously across the screen, but the voice in my head was louder than ever, a merciless, unforgiving critic tearing me apart.

"You should have known. You should have seen through it. How could you let this happen?"

By the time I was done, my body felt like an empty shell, drained of everything except a lingering, suffocating shame.

I did not know how to respond to his message. Until that moment, I had never experienced such an overwhelming, strange feeling, one that consumed me entirely.

I wished he were standing in front of me, so I could wrap my hands around his neck and squeeze until blood poured from his mouth. I wanted him to suffer, to endure unbearable pain, and I wanted to see every moment of it.

This was me—someone who, until that day, had never even harmed an ant. How could I, someone who once feared harming even an ant, wish for such destruction? The thought frightened me as much as the pain he had caused.

The agony inside me was unrelenting, like a fire that could burn through my skin, consuming everything in its path. Yet no remedy, no cure could soothe it.

I sat there for hours, crying until I felt completely drained, pouring out every ounce of my pain. Even in my sleep, the storm raged on, haunting me with visions I could not escape.

It was the middle of the night when I opened my eyes, the weight of restless dreams still lingering over me.

My thoughts raced as I replayed the past few days, piece by piece. I found myself going back to the very beginning, the moment I had left a comment on my favorite band's page.

Something urged me to check the comments again. I scrolled through them carefully, reading everyone. My heart sank as I stumbled upon several warnings: "Be cautious of scams! If anyone reaches out to you, it is fake. Do not fall for it."

"Report any suspicious accounts immediately."

And dozens of similar messages.

All of them had been posted just a day ago. It was clear now, I was not the only one. Others had been tricked too, lured in just as I had been.

I started reporting the account, over and over again, each click of the button a desperate attempt to regain some control. I needed to make sure it would be taken down and investigated. I needed justice, or at least the illusion of it.

Rage and hatred coursed through me like wildfire, burning away any remnants of reason. If money was all he wanted, why is he still playing this sick, twisted game with me? What else could he want? To humiliate me? To break me completely?

The questions came in waves, relentless and suffocating, each one cutting deeper than the last. My mind was a battlefield, torn between fury and despair. I could feel my heart pounding in my chest as if it were trying to escape the storm raging within me.

I clenched my fists, my nails digging into my palms, trying to anchor myself to the present. But it was no use—the questions, the betrayal, the disgust kept dragging me under like a whirlpool I could not escape.

The next day, I sent him a message, "Hello, my blue sky. I have missed you so much. I hope we can see each other soon."

I waited, my heart pounding, preparing myself for the battle ahead. I needed to know his next move, his true intentions.

A few minutes later, his reply arrived, "Hello, my sunshine. I have missed you too, darling. I was looking for your photos, but I could not find any. Why did you remove them? Is something wrong?"

His words were laced with fake concern, but I masked my anger and responded quickly, "No, darling, I just wanted you to miss me more. Maybe that way, you will hurry up and send the membership card so we can finally meet."

Plague: Oh, right! I forgot to tell you. My assistant said 500 dollars only converts to 200 euros. You should have sent at least 500 euros; otherwise, the card can't be issued.

A wave of fury swept through me, hotter and stronger than

before. My hands trembled as I typed back, "But I told you, my blue sky, that is all the money I have. You said you would cover the rest."

Plague: I cannot pay the rest with my card—I've already explained that. I had 1,000 euros in cash, which I used. I am not in a position to go to the bank.

Me: Isn't there something you can do? Please, I am begging you.

Plague: You do not understand my situation at all. I have done everything I could to see you, but you are not even willing to make an effort.

I clenched my teeth so hard it felt like they might shatter. His words, dripping with manipulation, cut through me like a dagger, tearing my soul apart.

My head throbbed painfully, and it felt as though my entire body was burning in the flames of my rage. His lies suffocated me, each word a knife twisting deeper into the wounds he had inflicted.

Plague: I have prepared everything for us to meet, a beautiful house in a stunning location. Even though I am in a tough situation and have to clear everything with my manager, I have taken this risk just to see you.

His words were like fuel to the fire burning within me. My anger, already simmering, flared with every word he typed.

Me: All right, darling. I will do whatever I can to see you.

Plague: I knew it, Sunshine. You truly are the gift the universe sent to me.

I clenched my jaw as I typed my next message, keeping my tone sweet and light.

Me: Darling, there is just one little condition.

I watched as the typing indicator flickered on and off for what felt like an eternity. He was hesitating, maybe even calculating. Finally, nothing came through.

Me: That last video you sent me, can you send it again? It got deleted after I watched it once.

Plague: I am not in a position to send a video right now. Why can't you understand that? Why are you asking me to resend it? Why does everyone expect so much from me?

His tone was sharp and defensive. It was obvious he was either genuinely angry or putting on an act to cover his tracks.

I took a deep breath, forcing myself to stay calm, masking my frustration with feigned affection.

Me: Darling, my blue sky, I miss you so much. I just want to see you again. Please send it, and I'll transfer the money right away and start packing my suitcase.

I added a string of heart and kiss emojis at the end of the message, my fingers trembling as I hit send.

Inside, my fury burned hotter than ever, but I knew I had to keep my mask intact. The game was not over yet, and I was not ready to lose.

During our conversation, Nelly called me several times, but I did not pick up. I knew that if I spoke to her, she would immediately sense the sorrow and pain I was trying so hard to hide.

Instead, I sent her a message, "I am fine, just cleaning my car right now. I will call you later."

It was easier to lie in a text than to let my voice betray me.

My hands were trembling so violently that even holding the phone felt like a challenge. The rage coursing through me was so intense, I could barely breathe. But somehow, I managed to write:

Me: Darling, I will send you a video of myself right now.

Plague: I have a request, too. I want to see my sunshine without clothes. I want to imagine you, bare and vulnerable, next to me tonight. You know, just for me. It would mean so much to feel closer to you tonight.

His words sent a wave of nausea through me, sharper than any pain I had ever known. It was as if every disgusting syllable poured gasoline onto the fire already raging within me. My hatred for him grew so intense, it felt like it might tear me apart.

With trembling hands and a heart pounding so hard, it echoed in my ears; I sent him the video Nelly had sent me.

Then, with the full force of my fury, I typed, each word cutting like a blade: You are the most despicable, vile creature I have ever met. You are not even human—you are filth, a bastard, a wretched excuse for existence. You are nothing but a plague, a sickness that destroys everything it touches.

Even as I sent the message, it did not feel like enough. My whole body burned with the intensity of my loathing. My teeth clenched, my breath came in shallow gasps, and it felt as though every muscle in my body was coiled, ready to explode. I was not just angry, I was consumed by the deepest hatred I had ever felt.

He kept typing and removing as if struggling to find the right words. In my mind, I could see his grotesque face, ugly, twisted, and filled with malice. I imagined his filthy hands, with blackened nails, moving across the keyboard. He was not just a liar; he was the embodiment of evil. He truly was the devil himself.

Finally, the message arrived.

Plague: You are the bastard, not me. I have been honest with you. Do you know how many people would kill to be in your place?

His audacity, his shamelessness, it made my stomach churn. Each word dripped with arrogance and lies.

I could not hold back. My fury erupted.

Me: Shut up. Shut up!

I typed it over and over, hammering the words into the screen as if they could somehow pierce through him.

Me: How could you do this to me? How could you pretend to be someone who, for me, was an icon of love and kindness? Was it all for money?

My anger burned hotter, but beneath it, pain tore through me like shards of glass. I could not stop myself.

Me: You killed me. You destroyed everything I believed in. You did not just shatter my heart, you destroyed my love, something that was a part of my soul, my spirit. Music and poetry.

Every word I typed felt like a desperate attempt to make him understand the depth of what he had taken from me. But deep down, I knew he would not care. People like him never did.

I blocked the account and removed everything I had saved from him. But nothing changed. The pain was still alive inside me, like a fire that refused to die out. I thought by erasing him; by removing all his memories, I would find peace, but I was wrong.

Amid all this, I received a message from an unfamiliar number, from an unknown place:

"Anna, please forgive me. I wanted to tell you everything,

but I could not. My conscience is tormenting me. Please, forgive me."

The message was repeated several times as if he wanted to carve every word into my mind. My heart raced, anger and confusion boiling within me. Then came a voice message—a shaky, remorseful voice of an unfamiliar man.

"Anna, I was influenced by my friend. He said we could make good money this way. But after talking to you, something changed. I liked you. Please, forgive me."

His voice was the voice of someone whose mask had been removed, but now it was too late.

My tears fell uncontrollably. Something about his voice did not make me feel better; on the contrary, it brought out even deeper anger and sadness. How could he dare? How could he so easily ask for my forgiveness after everything?

I stared at the screen, torn by conflicting emotions—rage, pain, and even a small part of me that wanted to believe his words. But that part could not overcome the wounds that had been inflicted on my soul.

He may have been remorseful, he may have apologized, but his apology did not undo the devastation he had caused. He had taken more than my heart, he had taken my belief, my trust, and even a part of my being.

I put the phone down, but his words still echoed in my mind. I felt broken, like someone standing in the middle of a storm, unsure of how to save themselves. I did not know what to do. I only knew that nothing would ever be the same again.

I did not know how to forgive him; it was as if I had forgotten what forgiveness even meant. I felt like a stranger to myself, as though I had become someone I no longer recognized. Tears, anger, and hatred consumed me, leaving no room for anything else.

Sitting on the floor, my arms wrapped tightly around my knees, I whispered to my father. If only he were here. At that moment, he was the only one who could have offered me solace, the only one who might have quieted the storm inside me.

I tilted my head toward the sky, tears streaming down my face, and murmured, "Father, where are you? You were the one who taught me how to love, but I wish you had taught me how to endure hate too. What am I supposed to do now, without you to guide me? How do I survive this emptiness?"

The silence that followed felt endless, the weight of my unanswered plea pressing down on me. For the first time, the sky itself felt distant, offering neither comfort nor hope.

The messages kept pouring in, relentless, desperate pleas for forgiveness. Each one felt like an echo of guilt and manipulation. My heart, as it always did, overpowered my mind. Against my better judgment, I typed back.

"I forgive you, but only on one condition—promise me you will never do this to anyone else again."

I did not wait for his response. I blocked him immediately.

But even after cutting him off, I was not free. The weight of it all bore down on me. Grief, anger, and self-blame churned inside me as I sat in silence, staring at nothing. The world felt too heavy, and I felt too small to carry it.

Chapter 9

The Final Goodbye

Then, my phone buzzed. It was Nelly.

For a moment, I hesitated, but I knew I had to answer. Forcing my voice to sound steady, I managed, "Hi, love. How are you?"

Nelly's cheerful tone was a sharp contrast to my despair.

"Hey, sis! How is everything? Are you okay? I just wanted to tell you I cannot make it for Christmas this year. I have decided to take on some extra shifts, the pay is too good to pass up. But do not worry! Once I have saved up a bit, we will plan a proper getaway. Just us. What do you think?"

Her excitement was contagious, but I could not muster the same energy. I forced a small smile, even though she could not see it, and said softly, "That sounds nice, Nelly. Let us do that."

Her optimism felt like a lifeline in the storm, but deep down, I wondered if I would ever find the strength to leave this darkness behind.

Nelly said with her usual excitement, "Sis, do not worry about a thing, okay? I have got it all figured out. I am planning to take you on the most amazing holiday!"

Her energy was contagious, and for a brief moment, it pulled me out of my dark thoughts. I loved her enthusiasm. Nelly was sharp, independent, and far more cautious than I ever was. Unlike me, who always trusted too easily, she was careful, never letting her guard down.

I thought to myself, I wish I could be like you. I wish I could see the world with both eyes wide open.

But I could not. I had always seen the world through a single lens, one that magnified its beauty while blurring its shadows. I saw only the light and ignored the darkness as if pretending it did not exist would make it disappear.

The reality, however, was far different. It was messy, cruel, and unforgiving. And now, sitting there, broken, and betrayed, I realised how blind I had been to the ugliness that had always been there, lurking in plain sight.

Nelly could tell something was wrong just from the tone of my voice. She did not press me with questions; instead, she launched into her usual cheerful chatter, quickly outlining her plans for the holiday. I knew she was trying to distract me, to lighten the weight I was carrying, but her words barely reached me.

I was trapped in a different world—a dark, suffocating abyss that felt endless. It was as though I was sinking into a deep, unrelenting swamp, with no hand strong enough to pull me out.

Even Nelly, with all her energy and optimism, could not reach the part of me that was breaking.

Her voice was like a distant echo, and though I appreciated her effort, I could not shake the feeling that I was completely alone, drowning in my own despair.

I said goodbye to Nelly and made a decision, I had to do something, anything, to feel better.

I turned on some music, hoping it would shift my mood. Music had always been my refuge, my escape. But now, it felt unbearable, like offering food to someone overcome with nausea. Each note twisted in my stomach, making me feel worse. I could not believe it. Music, the thing I loved most, had turned against me.

I kept switching songs, desperately searching for something, anything, that might soothe me. But nothing worked. I could not listen to a single melody without feeling the weight of my despair pressing down harder.

God, what has happened to me?

With unsteady steps, I walked toward my wardrobe. Every piece of clothing I had worn during those days, those moments of blissful delusion, now felt tainted, stained by memories I no longer wanted to keep. It was as if each item carried a trace of him, of his lies, of the hollow fantasies he had woven for me.

Without thinking, I pulled them off the hangers one by one, throwing them into a bag and tossing them aside. Yet nothing changed. The weight in my chest remained, like an old wound that refused to heal.

My eyes fell on my poetry journal, the notebook that had been my companion through countless days, each word a fragment of my soul. But now… now it felt meaningless, like words I could no longer believe in. With trembling hands, I tore out the pages, shredding them and scattering the pieces around me, as if with each torn fragment, I was trying to destroy a part of my memories.

But even that did not bring me peace. Standing there amidst the discarded clothes and the torn pages, I felt as though I was sinking deeper into a swamp, with nothing and no one to pull me out.

The next day, Nelly called me.

Nelly: "Hey, sis! How are you? I need a favor."

Me: "Hi, love. I'm okay. How about you? What do you need?"

"I want you to go to the bank and open a joint account for the two of us. I'll start depositing some money into it, so whenever you need cash, you can withdraw from it."

Me: "But I don't really need—"

Before I could finish, Nelly cut me off, as always. "Once you're there, message me so I can check what documents are required. Maybe I'll need to come too. Just ask what needs to be done. I'll be back by the end of the week, so don't forget to update me."

And with that, she ended the call.

Nelly never gave me much room to talk—she was always like that. Whatever she decided had to be done, no questions asked.

At the shopping center, I parked in the nearest spot to the entrance, hoping to make this as quick as possible. The bank was three floors up, and I stepped onto the escalator, feeling as if every second dragged on endlessly.

As I rose, I scanned the crowd around me, but instead of feeling like part of the bustling life, I felt utterly disconnected, like an outsider in a world that no longer made sense. Faces blurred into one another, each one looking strangely artificial, like poorly crafted masks hiding something sinister underneath.

A couple nearby was locked in a kiss, a sight that once might have seemed sweet or ordinary. But now, it only filled me with disgust. That kiss is fake, I thought bitterly. A lie, a performance meant to deceive. I wanted to scream at them, don't you see? Everything is a scam. Nothing is real.

Everyone around me felt like an imposter, a thief of something intangible—trust, innocence, belief. It was as if I had stepped into a masquerade, where beneath every smiling face lurked a hidden darkness. The world, once vibrant and full of life, now felt hollow, painted in dull shades of deception.

I arrived at the bank. It was a bit busy, but my turn came sooner than I expected. It was my first time at this branch, though Nelly had insisted that we open an account here. Knowing her, she probably had a specific plan in mind.

A polite, middle-aged staff member approached me with a friendly smile. He handed me a form to fill out and then led me to a separate room where the next steps would take place. The room had a large table with a computer, pens, notebooks, and various bank forms arranged on it. Several chairs were placed around the table, and he asked me to take a seat.

In front of me, there was a large television screen. The man explained that the account officer would assist me remotely through the screen, and I could ask any questions during the process.

Before he could finish his explanation, the screen flickered, and a young woman appeared, smiling warmly. She greeted me, and the man introduced me to her before quietly excusing himself from the room.

The woman introduced herself and started explaining the

process, but her words felt distant, like a hollow echo in a dark tunnel. She did not seem human anymore. To me, she was a twisted demon, something born from nightmares. Her face was marred by dark, festering patches, and her long, jagged teeth gleamed, each drop of blood dripping from them a silent threat. Her voice was not just a sound, it reverberated inside my skull, an eerie, otherworldly echo. Her tongue, grotesquely long and covered in harsh bristles, flicked out rhythmically, each time getting a little closer as if taunting me.

I tried to avoid her gaze, my eyes darting away, searching for anything else to focus on. I looked outside. The room's glass walls were covered in frosted designs, distorting the world beyond into a shadowy blur. Figures moved on the other side, but they were not people to me. They were shades, lifeless forms, like spirits caught between worlds—aimless, restless souls, circling the room in an endless loop, trapped in a grim dance of death.

I clenched my fists. I am not afraid of you. I am not afraid of her. I am not afraid of any of this. But my heart betrayed me, its frantic beats echoing in my ears. I could feel the fear creeping in, but I refused to let it take hold.

Raising my head, I fixed my eyes on the ceiling, imagining a sky beyond it: Something primal surged within me; rage, defiance, a desperate need to shatter the illusion around me. And then, before

I could think, I opened my mouth and released it all in a single scream.

It was not just a sound; it was a force. A raw, untamed cry, vibrant with purple intensity, ripped through the stillness of the room. It was not merely a scream, it was my rebellion against the shadows, the monsters, and the lies. It was my refusal to be broken.

The scream lingered in the air, like a living entity vibrating through the walls of my mind. For a moment, everything stopped. The demon-like woman froze mid-step, her crooked, jagged teeth bared in a grotesque grin. The shadows beyond the glass walls stood still, their endless circling broken, as though something had fractured the fabric of their dark world.

Then, a wave of energy surged through the room. It was faint at first, like ripples spreading across the surface of the water, but it grew stronger, resonating through the ground beneath my feet. The frosted designs on the glass walls began to melt away, revealing something more terrifying than I could have imagined, beyond the glass was no longer the outside world, but an infinite void filled with swirling violet and black mist, twisting like tangled branches.

The woman's form began to shift. Her grotesque appearance wavered like a mirage, and for a brief moment, her true self was revealed—a hollow-eyed figure cloaked in shadows, flickering like a dying flame. She let out a shrill cry, filled with both anger and fear.

"You shouldn't have done that," she whispered, each word laced with venom. Her long, twisted tongue flicked out again, but this time it recoiled as though burned by the force of my scream.

I took a step forward, emboldened by her reaction. The fear had not completely vanished, but something stronger had taken its place, a fierce, unyielding resolve.

"I'm not afraid of you anymore," I said, my voice steady, even though my heart was still pounding in my chest. "You're just another illusion, another lie."

The room began to tremble, cracks forming along the walls as the energy I had unleashed continued to surge. The glass shattered, shards falling like frozen raindrops into the void. The shadows dissolved into wisps of smoke; their endless dance was finally brought to an end.

The woman's eyes widened with something resembling fear. She took a step back, her distorted form flickering and becoming less real with each passing second. "This isn't over," she hissed, her voice warped, as though coming from some distant, dying world. "You've only just begun to see the truth."

Before I could respond, the ground beneath my feet gave way, and I fell—fell into the void beyond the shattered glass, the violet and black mists wrapping around me like cold tendrils.

But I was not afraid anymore. The fear that once held me captive had transformed into something else—freedom, defiance, and an unbreakable will to fight.

As I felt myself falling deeper into the void, a distant sound began to echo in my ears. It was faint at first like a whisper carried on the wind, but it gradually drew closer, becoming more distinct. The voice of the man, the employee, clear and dry, calling me back to reality.

I opened my eyes and took a deep breath. The dark world was gone. The room, with its glass walls and simple designs, had returned to normal. The man stood in front of me, his expression indifferent, waiting for me to listen. The haunting, surreal sensation had faded, but its imprint remained, quietly pulsing in my chest.

I quickly signed the forms and hurried toward my car. I did not want to see anyone; I felt disgusted by everything, by everyone, even by myself.

The heat outside was suffocating. I turned on the car's air conditioning and began driving toward home. An invisible weight pressed down on my chest, tightening around my throat. It was hard to breathe.

When I finally reached home and parked in the driveway, I did not get out right away. I sat there in silence, frozen in place. The pressure in my chest grew until the lump in my throat shattered, and tears streamed down my face.

I hated this feeling. I wanted to escape it, to free myself from this overwhelming sadness. But I did not know how.

I wished, more than anything, that I could go back in time and undo everything—make things right. But I felt powerless, as though my hands and feet were tied, trapped in a fate I could not control.

I leaned back against the seat, tilted my head up, and shouted into the emptiness above, "Why? Why me? What did I do wrong?"

Tears kept pouring down as I waited for an answer that would never come. For a few minutes, I stayed like that, lost in a storm of sorrow.

Finally, I reached out to turn off the air conditioning. My fingers accidentally brushed against the radio button, and it clicked on.

Suddenly, music began to fill the silent car:

"Chiquitita, tell me what is wrong

You are enchained by your own sorrow

In your eyes, there is no hope for tomorrow…"

I froze right there as if the universe were speaking to me.

The sound of the music filled the small space of the car, and each word felt like a fresh wound in my heart. But there was something in that song, something that calmed me, something that gave me hope.

"But the sun is still in the sky

And shining above you

Let me hear you sing once more

Like you did before

Sing a new song, Chiquitita…"

And then, a line that shone like a light piercing through the darkness echoed in my mind:

"You will shine once more…"

For a moment, I closed my eyes. Tears were still streaming down my face, but the suffocating weight I had felt before began to lift. It was as if something inside me had found a bit of peace, or perhaps the universe had just promised me that this feeling, this difficult moment, was only temporary, and one day, I would shine again.

I sat there in silence for a moment longer, the sound of the song still echoing in my mind. I was not okay, not yet—but something inside me had shifted. It was as if the universe had reminded me that, no matter how heavy today felt, I still had tomorrow. I did not have to fix everything now. I did not have to have all the answers. I just had to keep going.

I wiped my face and inhaled deeply, feeling the weight in my chest loosen, just a little. Outside, the sunlight danced on the leaves, and a soft breeze whispered through the air. Life has not stopped, it never does. And maybe that was the answer: to keep moving forward, one small step at a time.

As I started the engine, I whispered to myself,

"You will shine once more…"

Not as a promise, but as a quiet hope, a seed waiting to grow. And with that thought, I drove on, ready to begin again.

THE END

Life is always full of ups and downs. Sometimes you sink into deep despair, believing nothing can save you. But perhaps, in those very moments, something breaks the silence and gives you hope—a voice, a song, or even a quiet whisper from within that says: it is not over yet. You can still shine again.

Stay calm, my love

Watch the golden sparks of your stars,

See how your sky is filled with light.

Stay calm, my love

Do not fear, do not tremble,

Let those who wish to leave, go...

Not everything is lost.

Stay calm, my love

Even if the clocks remain silent,

In time, the bells will ring again.

Stay calm, my love

Open the parachute of your heart,

Trust in the gravity of love...

We will come rushing toward each other.

Stay calm, my love, stay calm...

We are the greater force,

The magic they call love.

Stay calm, my love, stay calm...

Love never changes,

And neither do we.

We pray for our love,

A light that will never fade.

Stay calm my love, stay calm

For to see the rainbow,

One must stand through the rain.

Stay calm, my love, stay calm.

A Letter to You, Who Thought You Had Won

Maybe you thought you deceived me, that you played with my emotions and drowned me in a false dream. Maybe, for a moment, you took pride in handing someone a hollow hope, only to shatter it mercilessly.

But today, as I write these words, not with anger, not with hatred, but with newfound understanding and a stronger heart—I want to tell you, Thank you.

Thank you for setting me on this path, even if your intention was deception.

Thank you for making me feel pain, because it was through those wounds that I was rebuilt.

Thank you for pushing me into darkness, because in that darkness, I found my own light.

You thought you took something from me, but in truth, you gave me something—A lesson no book could have ever taught me.

I learned that trust is a precious gem that should not be given away easily.

I learned that true love lies in honesty, not in beautifully crafted lies.

I learned that truth will always find its way through the veils of deception. And most importantly, I learned that I am stronger than any illusion. So today, I close this letter in peace—without resentment, without sorrow.

About The Author

Anita is a writer who dissolves the boundaries between reality and imagination. She believes that every story is a blend of truth and magic—a narrative born from real-life experiences, interwoven with the wonders of the unknown. For her, writing is not just an art; it is a bridge between the tangible world and undiscovered realms.

Her stories capture the deepest human emotions, inner journeys, and hidden mysteries that lie within the simplest moments of life. With every word that flows onto the page, the line between reality and fantasy blurs, inviting the reader on a journey where the possible and the impossible merge.

Every story holds a lesson within, a truth concealed in the shadows, waiting to be discovered by those who dare to see with the eyes of the heart. Yet, in the end, all these narratives remind us of one undeniable truth: within the depths of every reality, there lies a hidden magic, visible only to those who choose to look through the lens of imagination.

I was born in a land where borders are merely lines on a map, not walls between hearts. Skin color, gender, or nationality do not define us, for what connects us goes far beyond these differences. I am from you, and you are from me—we are all fragments of a greater whole. This bond, this shared humanity, is what gives life its meaning.

Let us love one another, for beyond every border and difference, we are one—reflections of a single soul in a thousand faces, fragments of a united light brought together on this journey of life. Love is the language that binds us beyond time and space, and only through it can the world return to its true essence.